I0020285

Jump Start Your Career
in Technology & IT
in about 100 Pages

Table of Contents

Let's Start !

About the Reviewers

Pedro Gomes is a technical manager at Critical Software. He is an expert on ASP.NET and SharePoint. He keeps a personal blog at http://blog.pedromvgomes.com and occasionally tweets as @pedromvgomes.

Marco Carreira is a software engineer at Critical Software. He excels at Windows Forms and sometimes can be seen cursing Entity Framework. Unfortunately, he has no blog (yet).

Tiago Andrade is a software developer at Sensefinity. He is particularly preeminent in Java and other legacy technologies.

Introduction

NHibernate Succinctly is a book for current and future NHibernate users. I expect that people with some degree of expertise (as well as newbies or wannabes) will be able to learn something from it. Like all *Succinctly* books, it follows a hands-on approach, so be prepared to see an extensive amount of C# code, XML, table diagrams, and so on.

Each chapter focuses on a concept—installing, configuring, querying, updating, extending, and common scenarios—and provides a realistic example. Throughout the book, I will give some practical advice, best practices, and guidance on how to avoid common pitfalls. In the end, my goal is to demonstrate that NHibernate is one of the most serious Object/Relational Mappers (ORMs) available—and one that deserves credibility.

All code samples are available for download on Syncfusion's repository at Bitbucket: https://bitbucket.org/syncfusiontech/nhibernate-succinctly. You will need at least Visual Studio 2010 installed and a SQL Server 2008 database in order to run the examples. However, it should be very easy to port to a different database; in fact, that's one of the reasons why we use NHibernate.

What is NHibernate and Why Should You Care?

NHibernate is one of the oldest Object/Relational Mappers (ORMs) available for the .NET world. But it still is relatively unknown to most developers, mostly because it has an aura of geekiness and complexity associated with it. But it's actually not that complex. Nowadays, ORMs are a hot topic and there are a lot of strong contenders. So, why pick NHibernate?

ORMs exist to fill a gap (or mismatch) between relational databases and object-oriented programming (OOP). For many OOP developers, knowing C# or some other object-oriented language is not the same as knowing SQL or database programming; their skills are usually stronger in OOP. With ORMs, you, the OOP developer, focus on what you know best: OOP code, and you do that in a database-independent way.

It also happens to be true that NHibernate has a number of features that are not commonly found in other ORMs. Take, for instance, the number of database engines that are supported out of the box. These include:

- Microsoft SQL Server, Microsoft SQL Server Compact edition (SQL CE), and Windows Azure SQL Database Object Linking and Embedding (OLE).
- Oracle.
- MySQL.
- Any database engine that supports Open Database Connectivity (ODBC) or Object Linking and Embedding Database (OLE DB).

Also, the ways by which its entities can be mapped and queried far exceeds those of its more direct contenders.

Realistically, we know that no API that tries to do everything will do everything well. NHibernate knows this, so it offers a number of extensibility points that you can use to make it better. Its API is incredibly powerful and can be used to extend even the slightest details including, for instance, the very SQL that is sent to perform all kinds of operations.

Let's start our journey!

Chapter 1 Installation

Before We Start

You will need a Visual Studio 2010/2012/2013 (any edition, including Express) and a SQL Server 2008 installation (any edition). The SQL Server instance must be using the TCP/IP protocol and must be accessible from the host where the examples will run. You will need permissions on the SQL Server to create a database; call it **Succinctly**.

Getting NHibernate

You can get NHibernate from a number of sources:

- NuGet.
- As source code from a GitHub repository.
- As a downloadable .zip package from SourceForge.

NuGet

On Visual Studio 2010/2012/2013, with an open .NET project, fire up the **Package Manager Console** and enter the following command:

```
PM> Install-Package NHibernate
```

This is probably the most convenient way to obtain NHibernate and to wire up references. It also allows you to update automatically when new versions are available. The NHibernate package will bring along **log4net** and **Iesi.Collections**; these are required dependencies (more on this later).

Figure 1: Manage NuGet Packages

By default, the package installer will only add references to the added packages in the current project, but you can add them explicitly to the other projects by clicking on **Manage NuGet Packages for Solution** and selecting the other projects:

Figure 2: Manage Packages for Solution

Downloadable Packages

There are packages available for download for current and past versions, including source code and reference documentation, on the SourceForge site at http://sourceforge.net/projects/nhibernate. Navigate to the **Files** page and select the version you want:

NHibernate

ayenderahien, fabiomaulo, julian-maughan, obergs, ricbrown, sbohlen

| Summary | Files | Reviews | Support | Wiki | Laconica | News | Code |

Looking for the latest version? Download NHibernate-3.3.3.CR1-bin.zip (8.7 MB)

Home / NHibernate / 3.3.2GA

Name ♦	Modified ♦	Size ♦	Downloads ♦
↑ Parent folder			
NHibernate-3.3.2.GA-src.zip	2012-10-22	18.2 MB	27
NHibernate-3.3.2.GA-reference.zip	2012-10-22	1.6 MB	17
NHibernate-3.3.2.GA-bin.zip	2012-10-22	8.7 MB	39
Totals: 3 Items		28.4 MB	83

Figure 3: NHibernate Project at SourceForge

Download the binary distribution (the one ending in **.bin**), extract the files into a local folder, and add references to the DLLs **NHibernate.dll**, **Iesi.Collections.dll**, and **log4net.dll** to your projects so that you can start using NHibernate right away.

Source Code

The NHibernate source code repository can be found on GitHub under the name **nhibernate-core**. You need to install a Git client (which you can download from http://git-scm.com) and clone this repository into your local drive. Using the command line, it would look something like this:

```
Administrator: Visual Studio x64 Win64 Command Prompt (2010)
Setting environment for using Microsoft Visual Studio 2010 x64 tools.

C:\>cd Source

C:\Source>git clone git://github.com/nhibernate/nhibernate-core.git
Cloning into 'nhibernate-core'...
remote: Counting objects: 83890, done.
remote: Compressing objects: 100% (17330/17330), done.
remote: Total 83890 (delta 66587), reused 82943 (delta 65786)
Receiving objects: 100% (83890/83890), 51.50 MiB | 63 KiB/s, done.
Resolving deltas: 100% (66587/66587), done.

C:\Source>
```

Figure 4: Cloning the NHibernate GitHub Repository

There's a web interface for this repository available at https://github.com/nhibernate/nhibernate-core where you see the latest changes, browse through the folders, and view individual files including their content and individual changes.

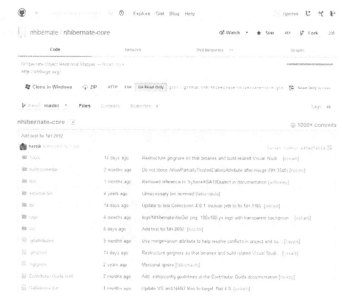

Figure 5: NHibernate Project's GitHub Web Interface

Once you have the files locally, enter the **nhibernate-core** folder and run the **ShowBuildMenu.bat** script:

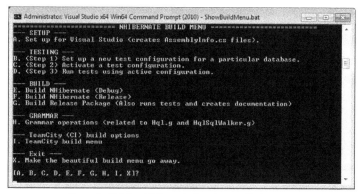

Figure 6: Building NHibernate from Source Code

When you run this script for the first time, you need to first select option **A** for setting up the Visual Studio files. This is only needed once; afterwards, to obtain a build package, either choose option **E** or **F** for **Debug** or **Release** builds. After the build process terminates, binaries will be available on the **nhibernate-core\build\<version>** folder and you can add them as references to your projects.

There are some things you should keep in mind when using the source code repository:

- You can get the latest changes at any time by running **git pull**.

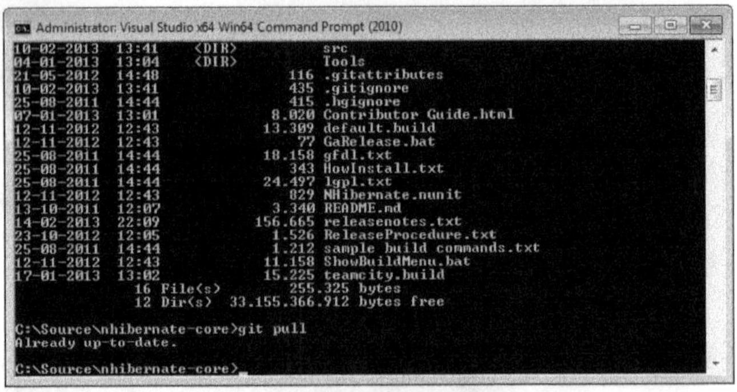

Figure 7: Getting Latest Changes

- The files you are obtaining are the latest unstable ones; that is, they are the result of individual contributions and experimental features as soon as they are submitted, and may not be so thoroughly tested as the official packages (the ones you get from NuGet or SourceForge).
- You are free to experiment and make modifications to the local source code files. Don't be alarmed; you can always revert if something goes wrong. Or you can implement some new functionality or fix some bugs, in which case you may want to make these modifications available to everyone using NHibernate. More on this in the last chapter, **Additional References**.

What's Inside

The NHibernate binary distribution consists of three files: **Nhibernate.dll**, **Iesi.Collections.dll**, and **log4net.dll**. Some explanation about their purpose is as follows:

- **NHibernate.dll** contains the core NHibernate libraries; these are the ones you need to work with NHibernate. This is a .NET 3.5 assembly which, as you probably know, is basically .NET 2.0 with some additional libraries and support for LINQ syntax. Thanks to backwards compatibility, NHibernate still targets .NET 2.0 (which doesn't mean you can't use it in a .NET 4.0 or .NET 4.5 project because, indeed, you can).
- **Iesi.Collections.dll** contains some collection definitions and implementations that, as of .NET 2.0/3.5, didn't exist in the .NET Base Class Library. The most notable of these is a

set interface and some implementations; the **NHibernate.dll** internally makes use of this assembly and most likely you will, too, so it must also be present. Its source code is together with NHibernate's.

- **log4net.dll** is actually an external project; you can find its home page at http://logging.apache.org/log4net and, if you don't know, it's a general purpose logger. Internally, NHibernate uses log4net for its own logging including runtime warnings, debug messages, exceptions, and generated SQL queries. Although strictly not required–NHibernate will detect whether log4net is present at startup and won't complain if it is not–it may be very useful, especially when debugging your projects. Of course, log4net is a very mature library used in several projects and you may also be interested in using it for your own logging purposes.

Which One Shall I Choose?

It is up to you which one you choose but I would recommend NuGet due to its simplicity and ease of use. On the other hand, if you want to live dangerously and stay up to date with the latest development on the NHibernate core, by all means, use the source!

Chapter 2 Configuration

Before using NHibernate, you must configure it. Basic required configuration consists of the database driver, the dialect to use, and the driver-specific database connection string. As you will see, there are several ways to make this configuration in NHibernate.

For the drivers and dialects, these are the ones included with NHibernate:

NHibernate Drivers and Dialects

Driver	Dialects	Description
CsharpSqliteDriver	GenericDialect	A NHibernate driver for the Community CsharpSqlite data provider
DB2400Driver	DB2400Dialect	A NHibernate driver for using the IBM.Data.DB2.iSeries data provider
DB2Driver	DB2Dialect	A NHibernate driver for using the IBM.Data.DB2 data provider
FirebirdClientDriver	FirebirdDialect	A NHibernate driver for using the Firebird data provider located in FirebirdSql.Data.FirebirdClient assembly
FirebirdDriver	FirebirdDialect	A NHibernate driver for using the FirebirdSql.Data.Firebird data provider
IfxDriver	InformixDialect InformixDialect0940 InformixDialect1000	A NHibernate driver for using the Informix data provider
IngresDriver	IngresDialect	A NHibernate driver for using the Ingres data provider

Driver	Dialects	Description
MySqlDataDriver	MySQLDialect MySQL5Dialect	Provides a database driver for MySQL
NpgsqlDriver	PostgreSQLDialect PostgreSQL81Dialect PostgreSQL82Dialect	The PostgreSQL data provider provides a database driver for PostgreSQL
OdbcDriver	GenericDialect	A NHibernate driver for using the ODBC Data Provider
OleDbDriver	GenericDialect	A NHibernate driver for using the OleDb Data Provider
OracleClientDriver	Oracle8iDialect Oracle9iDialect Oracle10gDialect	A NHibernate driver for using the Oracle Data Provider
OracleDataClientDriver	Oracle8iDialect Oracle9iDialect Oracle10gDialect	A NHibernate driver for using the Oracle.DataAccess data provider
OracleLiteDataClientDriver	OracleLiteDialect	A NHibernate driver for using the Oracle.DataAccess.Lite data provider
Sql2008ClientDriver	MsSql2008Dialect MsSqlAzure2008Dialect	SQL Server 2008 and Azure driver
SqlClientDriver	MsSql7Dialect MsSql2000Dialect	A NHibernate driver for using the SqlClient data provider

Driver	Dialects	Description
	MsSql2005Dialect	
SQLite20Driver	SQLiteDialect	NHibernate driver for the System.Data.SQLite data provider for .NET 2.0
SqlServerCeDriver	MsSqlCeDialect MsSqlCe40Dialect	A NHibernate driver for Microsoft SQL Server CE data provider
SybaseAsaClientDriver	SybaseASA9Dialect	The SybaseAsaClientDriver driver provides a database driver for Adaptive Server Anywhere 9.0
SybaseAseClientDriver	SybaseASE15Dialect	This provides a driver for Sybase ASE 15 using the ADO.NET driver
SybaseSQLAnywhereDot Net4Driver	SybaseSQLAnywhere1 0Dialect	SQL Dialect for SQL Anywhere 12
SybaseSQLAnywhereDriv er	SybaseSQLAnywhere1 0Dialect SybaseSQLAnywhere1 1Dialect	The SybaseSQLAnywhereDriver Driver provides a database driver for Sybase SQL Anywhere 10 and above

Some of these drivers and dialects are subclasses of others, which means they inherit something from their ancestors as well as add something new. You are free to create your own classes by inheriting from the most appropriate one.

A driver is the class responsible by actually creating the connection, by instancing a **System.Data.Common.DbConnection**-derived class suitable for a particular database engine. If you have ODBC or OLE DB drivers available, you can connect to virtually any database by using the corresponding NHibernate drivers (but you will have better performance if you use a specific driver).

The dialect describes characteristics and registers functions of a specific version of an engine so, generally speaking, you should choose the dialect that is closer to the actual version you are using (although you can always use the generic dialect).

A configuration is, essentially, an instance of the **NHibernate.Cfg.Configuration** class. It needs to get populated somehow and is required for using NHibernate since everything starts from it. You may have several configuration instances, which is typical if you need to support different databases at the same time (even hosted in different engines). In most cases, however, you will need only one configuration instance.

XML Configuration

In previous versions of NHibernate, the only possible configuration was through XML. The process now is: you register a custom section on the configuration file (**App.config** or **Web.config**) and you create this section, filling its required definitions. This section would look like this:

```xml
<?xml version="1.0" encoding="utf-8" ?>
<configuration>
  <configSections>
    <section name="hibernate-configuration"
type="NHibernate.Cfg.ConfigurationSectionHandler, NHibernate" />
  </configSections>
  <hibernate-configuration xmlns="urn:nhibernate-configuration-2.2">
    <session-factory>
      <property name="hbm2ddl.keywords">auto-quote</property>

<property name="connection.driver_class">NHibernate.Driver.Sql2008ClientDriv
er
      </property>

<property name="dialect">NHibernate.Dialect.MsSql2008Dialect</property>

        <property name="connection.connection_string_name">Succinctly</prope
rty>
        <property name="query.substitutions">true 1, false 0</property>
      <mapping assembly="Succinctly.Model" />
    </session-factory>
  </hibernate-configuration>
  <connectionStrings>
    <add name="Succinctly" providerName="System.Data.SqlClient"
connectionString="Data Source=. \sqlexpress; Integrated Security=SSPI; Initi
al Catalog=Succinctly"/>
  </connectionStrings>
</configuration>
```

This is a minimal NHibernate configuration. You can see that inside the **hibernate-configuration** section we are setting some properties and adding a mapping reference. Their meaning is:

- **hbm2ddl.keywords**: Tells NHibernate if it should automatically escape all column and table names so that, if reserved keywords are used, they are treated appropriately. For example, in SQL Server, replace any column named **INT** for **[INT]**, **ORDER** for **[ORDER]**, etc. Although not required, it is very handy to have this setting. I advise you to keep it.

- **connection.driver_class**: The full name of a .NET class that implements a NHibernate driver and thus allows you to connect to a database (see the above table). In this example, we are using the SQL Server 2008 driver; this is a required property.
- **dialect**: Also a required setting for the full name of a .NET class that is tied to the driver and supports a specific database version's dialect. For this example, we will be using the SQL Server 2008.
- **connection.connection_string_name**: The name of a connection string specified in its own section (**connectionStrings**); this is required unless you set the actual connection string in a property **connection.connection_string**. It is recommended that you leave the connection strings on their own section and just reference the one you want by its unique name (in this case, **Succinctly**).
- **query.substitutions**: Some constant substitutions that will be performed whenever a query is about to be sent to the database. In this example, we are translating the string constants **true** and **false** for their SQL Server equivalents, **1** and **0**, respectively. Although strictly not required, you should have this setting or you may run into trouble when executing HQL queries.

mapping: The full name of an assembly containing entity classes and their mapping files, using XML configuration for this purpose (more on this on the Chapter 3 Domain Model

Scenario

Let's consider a simple model, a blogging system:

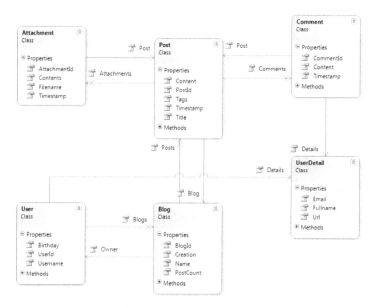

Figure 8: Class Model for a Blogging System

It can be described as this: A **Blog** is owned by a **User** and has a collection of **Posts**. Each **Post** may have **Comments** and **Attachments**, each referring to a single **Post**. A **User** may have several **Blogs**. Both **User** and **Comment** have **UserDetails**.

Occasionally, I will also refer another model, a classical ordering system, which will look like this:

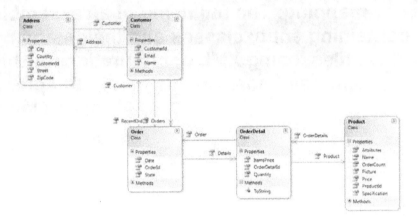

Figure 9: Class Model for the Orders System

These are the concepts that we will want to represent and manipulate in our code. However, I will only include code for the blogging model. You will be able to find the classes and mappings for the ordering model on the book's Bitbucket repository.

Entities

We have several ways to represent these concepts. I chose one. Here are the classes that we will be using throughout the book:

The **User** class:

```csharp
public class User
{
  public User()
  {
    this.Blogs = new Iesi.Collections.Generic.HashedSet<Blog>();
    this.Details = new UserDetail();
  }

  public virtual Int32 UserId { get; protected set;}

  public virtual String Username { get; set; }

  public virtual UserDetail Details { get; set; }

  public virtual DateTime? Birthday { get; set; }

  public virtual Iesi.Collections.Generic.ISet<Blog> Blogs { get;
protected set; }
}
```

The **Blog** class:

```
public class Blog
{
  public Blog()
  {
    this.Posts = new List<Post>();
  }

  public virtual Int32 BlogId { get; protected set; }

  public virtual System.Drawing.Image Picture { get; set; }

  public virtual Int64 PostCount { get; protected set; }

  public virtual User Owner { get; set; }

  public virtual String Name { get; set; }

  public virtual DateTime Creation { get; set; }

  public virtual IList<Post> Posts { get; protected set; }
}
```

💡 *Tip: Because the Blog class has a property of type* System.Drawing.Image, *you need to add a reference to the* System.Drawing *assembly.*

The **Post** class:

```
public class Post
{
  public Post()
  {
    this.Tags = new Iesi.Collections.Generic.HashedSet<String>();
    this.Attachments = new Iesi.Collections.Generic.HashedSet<Attachment>();
    this.Comments = new List<Comment>();
  }

  public virtual Int32 PostId { get; protected set; }

  public virtual Blog Blog { get; set; }

  public virtual DateTime Timestamp { get; set; }

  public virtual String Title { get; set; }

  public virtual String Content { get; set; }

  public virtual Iesi.Collections.Generic.ISet<String> Tags { get;
protected set; }

  public virtual Iesi.Collections.Generic.ISet<Attachment> Attachments {
get; protected set; }
```

```
    public virtual IList<Comment> Comments { get; protected set; }
}
```

The **Comment** class:

```
public class Comment
{
  public Comment()
  {
    this.Details = new UserDetail();
  }

  public virtual Int32 CommentId { get; protected set; }

  public virtual UserDetail Details { get; set; }

  public virtual DateTime Timestamp { get; set; }

  public virtual String Content { get; set; }

  public virtual Post Post { get; set; }
}
```

The **Attachment** class:

```
public class Attachment
{
  public virtual Int32 AttachmentId { get; protected set; }

  public virtual String Filename { get; set; }

  public virtual Byte[] Contents { get; set; }

  public virtual DateTime Timestamp { get; set; }

  public virtual Post Post { get; set; }
}
```

And, finally, the **UserDetail** class (it is the implementation of the **Details** component of the **User** and **Comment** classes):

```
public class UserDetail
{
  public String Url { get; set; }

  public String Fullname { get; set; }

  public String Email { get; set; }
}
```

Some notes:

- As you can see, there is no base class or special interface that we need to implement. This does not mean that NHibernate can't use them; it is actually quite the opposite.
- All classes are non-sealed. This is not strictly a requirement but a recommended practice.
- Some properties are virtual, basically all except those from the **UserDetail** component class. Also, a recommended practice; we will see why when we talk about lazy loading in the next chapter.
- Properties that will represent the primary key have a protected setter. This is because NHibernate will be providing this key for us so there is no need. In fact, it is dangerous to change it.
- Collections also have protected setters because the operations that we will be performing with them won't require changing the actual collection reference, but rather, merely adding, removing, and eventually clearing it.
- All collections are instantiated in the constructor of their declaring classes so that they are never **null**.

Before We Start

Because NHibernate is an ORM, it will transform tables into classes, columns into properties, and records into object instances and values. Exactly how this transformation occurs depends on the mapping. A mapping is something that you add to the configuration instance. You can add multiple mappings—typically one for each .NET class that you want to be able to persist to the database. At the very minimum, a mapping must associate a table name to a class name, the column that contains the primary key to a related class property, and probably some additional columns into the properties they will be turned to.

As far as NHibernate is concerned, an entity is just a Plain Old CLR Object (POCO). You have to make a fundamental choice when it comes to creating these entities:

- You start from code, following a Domain Driven Design (DDD) approach. You define your classes without much concern about how they will be stored in the database. Instead, you focus on getting them right. This may include creating inheritance relationships and complex properties.
- You start from the database and you have to craft your entities so that they match the data model. This may be because it's the way your company works, you have a legacy database, or it is just a matter of personal preference.

We won't go into what is the best approach; that is up to you. Either way is fully supported by NHibernate. If you start from code, NHibernate will happily generate the database for you or validate it. In both cases—database first or code first—NHibernate will also give you the option to check the database against your entities and either update the database to match the entities or warn you if there are discrepancies. There's a **SchemaAction** setting for this on the **Configuration** class, using loquacious configuration:

```
Configuration cfg = new Configuration()
.DataBaseIntegration(db =>
{
    //...
    db.SchemaAction = SchemaAutoAction.Validate;
```

```
})
```

As well as in XML configuration, as a property:

```
<property name="hbm2ddl.auto">validate</property>
```

The possible values you can pass to **SchemaAction/hbm2ddl.auto** are:

- **Create/create**: Will always drop existing tables and recreate them from the current mappings.
- **Recreate/create-drop**: Identical to **Create,** with the difference being that it will drop everything again when NHibernate finishes using the database (the session factory is disposed of).
- **Update/update**: NHibernate will compare the existing tables to the current mappings and will update the database, if necessary, including creating missing tables or columns.
- **Validate/validate**: An exception will be thrown if the comparison between the actual tables and the current mapping detects mismatches.

 Tip: Create and Recreate are dangerous, and you should only use them for scenarios such as unit tests or demonstrations where you need to quickly set up a database or where you have no important information because every mapped table will be dropped—not mapped tables will be left alone, though. Update will also create any missing tables and columns so it is safe to use in real-life scenarios, but it may take some time to check all tables if you have a lot of mapped classes. If no value is set by calling SchemaAction or by setting the hbm2ddl.auto attribute on the XML configuration, no validation will be performed and no schema update/creation will occur.

Chapter 4 Mappings chapter). It is not required as there are other ways to achieve this. But, nonetheless, it is useful and you can place as many mapping entries as you want.

To build the configuration instance and load settings from the configuration file, all you need is:

```
Configuration cfg = new Configuration().Configure();
```

 Tip: Import the NHibernate.Cfg namespace.

If you would like to use XML-based configuration, one thing that may come in handy is Visual Studio IntelliSense. You can add such support by following the following steps:

Download the XML Schema Definition (XSD) file for the configuration section from https://github.com/nhibernate/nhibernate-core/blob/master/src/NHibernate/nhibernate-configuration.xsd.

Open the Web.config or App.config file where you have the NHibernate configuration in Visual Studio.

Go to the Properties window and select the ellipsis (...) button next to Schemas.

Click the Add... button and select the nhibernate-configuration.xsd file that you just downloaded.

Select Use this Schema at the line with target namespace urn:nhibernate-configuration-2.2:

urn:Microsoft.VisualStudio.Data.Schema.Permissions	Microsoft.VisualStudio.Data.Schema.Permissions.xsd	C:\Program Files (
urn:Microsoft.VisualStudio.Data.Tools.Permissions	Microsoft.VisualStudio.Data.Tools.Permissions.xsd	C:\Program Files (
✓ ⬇ urn:nhibernate-configuration-2.2	nhibernate-configuration.xsd	C:\Program Files (
Automatic pping-2.2	nhibernate-mapping.xsd	C:\Program Files (
Use this schema dator-1.0	nhv-mapping.xsd	C:\Program Files (
✕ Do not use this schema ion-1.0	nhv-configuration.xsd	C:\Program Files (
urn:schemas-microsoft-com:datatypes	xdrtypes.xsd	C:\Program Files (
urn:schemas-microsoft-com:rowset	XdrRowset.xsd	C:\Program Files (

XML Schemas for IntelliSense

When you close the XML Schemas window, you will have IntelliSense:

IntelliSense for NHibernate XML

Loquacious Configuration

NHibernate 3.2 brought along what is called loquacious (or fluent) configuration. Basically, it renders the configuration section on the configuration file unnecessary and, instead, relies on code to initialize NHibernate. The configuration expressed in the previous section can be transformed into the following code:

```
Configuration cfg = new Configuration()
```

```
.DataBaseIntegration(db =>

{

  db.ConnectionStringName = "Succinctly";

  db.Dialect<MsSql2008Dialect>();

  db.Driver<Sql2008ClientDriver>();

  db.HqlToSqlSubstitutions = "true 1, false 0";

  db.KeywordsAutoImport = Hbm2DDLKeyWords.AutoQuote;

})

.AddAssembly("NHibernate.Succinctly");
```

> 💡 **Tip: You will need to import the NHibernate, NHibernate.Cfg, NHibernate.Dialect, and NHibernate.Driver namespaces.**

Some things worth mentioning:

- The Dialect and Driver methods take generic parameters that must inherit from NHibernate.Dialect.Dialect and implement NHibernate.Driver.IDriver, respectively. As such, there is no easy way to pass in dynamically resolved types, for example, of type System.Type or in string format. For that, you can use the equivalent properties dialect and connection.driver_class:

```
Configuration cfg = BuildConfiguration()//whatever way you like

.SetProperty(NHibernate.Cfg.Environment.ConnectionDriver, typeof(Sql2008Clie
ntDriver)

.AssemblyQualifiedName)

.SetProperty(NHibernate.Cfg.Environment.Dialect, typeof(MsSql2008Dialect).As
semblyQualifiedName)
```

- The **AddAssembly** method also has an overload that takes an **Assembly** instance.
- If you have both a configuration section and loquacious configuration, loquacious settings take precedence.

Which One Shall I Choose?

Again, which one you choose is up to you. They are fundamentally equivalent. XML-based configuration offers you the advantage of allowing changes without requiring recompilation of the code. However, it merely delays eventual configuration errors to a later stage when the application is run. Loquacious configuration, on the other hand, may detect syntactic errors sooner—even preventing the code from compiling altogether—at the cost of requiring recompilation just to make even the smallest change. But it allows conditional configuration, something you can't achieve with static XML. You can have the best of both worlds and have both XML-based as well as by code configuration in the same project. It may make sense if, for example, you have to deal with legacy **HBM.XML** files.

These are the most basic settings required for NHibernate to work. Most of this book's examples are agnostic regarding which database engine is used. Whenever this is not the case, it will be explicitly mentioned. Later on we will learn functionality that will require additional settings and so we will come back to this.

 Note: It is also possible to have the configuration entries in an external file; that is, not as content inside the App.config *or* Web.config *files or even as a resource embedded in some assembly. These are not typical scenarios and won't be covered here, but you are free to explore them by looking at the various overloads of the* Configuration.Configure *method.*

Chapter 3 Domain Model

Scenario

Let's consider a simple model, a blogging system:

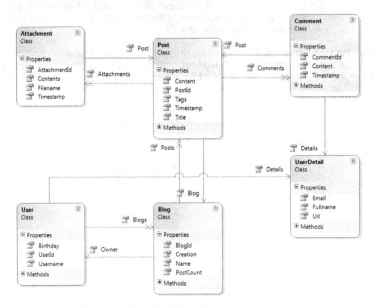

Figure 10: Class Model for a Blogging System

It can be described as this: A **Blog** is owned by a **User** and has a collection of **Posts**. Each **Post** may have **Comments** and **Attachments**, each referring to a single **Post**. A **User** may have several **Blogs**. Both **User** and **Comment** have **UserDetails**.

Occasionally, I will also refer another model, a classical ordering system, which will look like this:

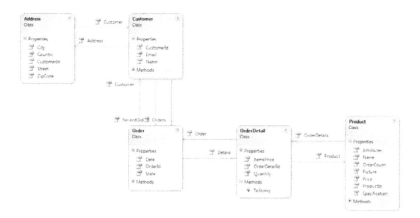

Figure 11: Class Model for the Orders System

These are the concepts that we will want to represent and manipulate in our code. However, I will only include code for the blogging model. You will be able to find the classes and mappings for the ordering model on the book's Bitbucket repository.

Entities

We have several ways to represent these concepts. I chose one. Here are the classes that we will be using throughout the book:

The **User** class:

```
public class User
{
  public User()
  {
    this.Blogs = new Iesi.Collections.Generic.HashedSet<Blog>();
    this.Details = new UserDetail();
  }

  public virtual Int32 UserId { get; protected set;}

  public virtual String Username { get; set; }

  public virtual UserDetail Details { get; set; }

  public virtual DateTime? Birthday { get; set; }

  public virtual Iesi.Collections.Generic.ISet<Blog> Blogs { get;
protected set; }
}
```

The **Blog** class:

```
public class Blog
{
    public Blog()
    {
        this.Posts = new List<Post>();
    }

    public virtual Int32 BlogId { get; protected set; }

    public virtual System.Drawing.Image Picture { get; set; }

    public virtual Int64 PostCount { get; protected set; }

    public virtual User Owner { get; set; }

    public virtual String Name { get; set; }

    public virtual DateTime Creation { get; set; }

    public virtual IList<Post> Posts { get; protected set; }
}
```

> *Tip: Because the Blog class has a property of type* System.Drawing.Image, *you need to add a reference to the* System.Drawing *assembly.*

The **Post** class:

```
public class Post
{
    public Post()
    {
        this.Tags = new Iesi.Collections.Generic.HashedSet<String>();
        this.Attachments = new Iesi.Collections.Generic.HashedSet<Attachment>();
        this.Comments = new List<Comment>();
    }

    public virtual Int32 PostId { get; protected set; }

    public virtual Blog Blog { get; set; }

    public virtual DateTime Timestamp { get; set; }

    public virtual String Title { get; set; }

    public virtual String Content { get; set; }

    public virtual Iesi.Collections.Generic.ISet<String> Tags { get;
protected set; }

    public virtual Iesi.Collections.Generic.ISet<Attachment> Attachments {
get; protected set; }
```

```
    public virtual IList<Comment> Comments { get; protected set; }
}
```

The **Comment** class:

```
public class Comment
{
    public Comment()
    {
        this.Details = new UserDetail();
    }

    public virtual Int32 CommentId { get; protected set; }

    public virtual UserDetail Details { get; set; }

    public virtual DateTime Timestamp { get; set; }

    public virtual String Content { get; set; }

    public virtual Post Post { get; set; }
}
```

The **Attachment** class:

```
public class Attachment
{
    public virtual Int32 AttachmentId { get; protected set; }

    public virtual String Filename { get; set; }

    public virtual Byte[] Contents { get; set; }

    public virtual DateTime Timestamp { get; set; }

    public virtual Post Post { get; set; }
}
```

And, finally, the **UserDetail** class (it is the implementation of the **Details** component of the **User** and **Comment** classes):

```
public class UserDetail
{
    public String Url { get; set; }

    public String Fullname { get; set; }

    public String Email { get; set; }
}
```

Some notes:

- As you can see, there is no base class or special interface that we need to implement. This does not mean that NHibernate can't use them; it is actually quite the opposite.
- All classes are non-sealed. This is not strictly a requirement but a recommended practice.
- Some properties are virtual, basically all except those from the **UserDetail** component class. Also, a recommended practice; we will see why when we talk about lazy loading in the next chapter.
- Properties that will represent the primary key have a protected setter. This is because NHibernate will be providing this key for us so there is no need. In fact, it is dangerous to change it.
- Collections also have protected setters because the operations that we will be performing with them won't require changing the actual collection reference, but rather, merely adding, removing, and eventually clearing it.
- All collections are instantiated in the constructor of their declaring classes so that they are never **null**.

Before We Start

Because NHibernate is an ORM, it will transform tables into classes, columns into properties, and records into object instances and values. Exactly how this transformation occurs depends on the mapping. A mapping is something that you add to the configuration instance. You can add multiple mappings—typically one for each .NET class that you want to be able to persist to the database. At the very minimum, a mapping must associate a table name to a class name, the column that contains the primary key to a related class property, and probably some additional columns into the properties they will be turned to.

As far as NHibernate is concerned, an entity is just a Plain Old CLR Object (POCO). You have to make a fundamental choice when it comes to creating these entities:

- You start from code, following a Domain Driven Design (DDD) approach. You define your classes without much concern about how they will be stored in the database. Instead, you focus on getting them right. This may include creating inheritance relationships and complex properties.
- You start from the database and you have to craft your entities so that they match the data model. This may be because it's the way your company works, you have a legacy database, or it is just a matter of personal preference.

We won't go into what is the best approach; that is up to you. Either way is fully supported by NHibernate. If you start from code, NHibernate will happily generate the database for you or validate it. In both cases—database first or code first—NHibernate will also give you the option to check the database against your entities and either update the database to match the entities or warn you if there are discrepancies. There's a **SchemaAction** setting for this on the **Configuration** class, using loquacious configuration:

```
Configuration cfg = new Configuration()
.DataBaseIntegration(db =>
{
    //...
    db.SchemaAction = SchemaAutoAction.Validate;
```

```
})
```

As well as in XML configuration, as a property:

```
<property name="hbm2ddl.auto">validate</property>
```

The possible values you can pass to **SchemaAction/hbm2ddl.auto** are:

- **Create/create**: Will always drop existing tables and recreate them from the current mappings.
- **Recreate/create-drop**: Identical to **Create,** with the difference being that it will drop everything again when NHibernate finishes using the database (the session factory is disposed of).
- **Update/update**: NHibernate will compare the existing tables to the current mappings and will update the database, if necessary, including creating missing tables or columns.
- **Validate/validate**: An exception will be thrown if the comparison between the actual tables and the current mapping detects mismatches.

 Tip: Create and Recreate are dangerous, and you should only use them for scenarios such as unit tests or demonstrations where you need to quickly set up a database or where you have no important information because every mapped table will be dropped—not mapped tables will be left alone, though. Update will also create any missing tables and columns so it is safe to use in real-life scenarios, but it may take some time to check all tables if you have a lot of mapped classes. If no value is set by calling SchemaAction or by setting the hbm2ddl.auto attribute on the XML configuration, no validation will be performed and no schema update/creation will occur.

Chapter 4 Mappings

Concepts

We essentially define mappings for:

- Entities.
- Entity identifiers.
- Entity properties.
- References to other entities.
- Collections.
- Inheritance.

Identifiers, properties, references, and collections are all members of the entity class where:

- Identifiers can either be of simple .NET types, such as those one would find as table columns (such as **Int32**, **String** or **Boolean**), but also common value types such as **DateTime**, **Guid** or **TimeSpan** or, for representing composite primary keys, they can also be of some custom class type.
- Scalar properties (or just properties) are also of primitive or common value types; other cases are **Byte[]** for generic Binary Large Objects (BLOBs) and **XDocument/XmlDocument** for XML data types.
- Complex properties, known as value objects in Domain-Driven Design (DDD) and as components in NHibernate, are classes with some properties that are logically grouped together. Think of a postal address, for example, which may be comprised of a street address, zip code, city, country, etc. Of course, in the database, these are also stored as scalar columns.
- References to other entities (one-to-one, many-to-one) are declared as the type of the entity in the other endpoint of the relation; in the database, these are foreign key columns.
- Collections of entities (one-to-many, many-to-many) are declared as collections of the other endpoint's entity type. Of course, in the database these are also stored as foreign key columns.

Let's look at each of these concepts in more detail.

Entities

An entity is at the core of a NHibernate mapping. It is a .NET class that will be saved into one (or more, as we will see) table. Its most important configurable options are:

- Name: The name of the class; a mandatory setting.
- Table: The table to which the class is mapped, also a mandatory setting unless we are defining a hierarchy of classes

- Laziness: If the entity's class allows creating a proxy to it, thus allowing lazy loading. The default is **true**.
- Mutable: If any changes to the class' members should be persisted to the database. The default is **true**.
- Optimistic lock: The strategy to be followed for optimistic concurrency control (see Optimistic). The default is **none**.
- Where restriction: An optional SQL restriction (see Restrictions).
- Batch size: The number of additional instances of the same type that will be loaded automatically by NHibernate. It is not a required setting and the default value is **0**.

Properties

A property either maps to a column in a table or to a SQL formula, in which case it will not be persisted but instead calculated when the containing entity is loaded from the database. A property has the following attributes:

- Name: The name of the property in the entity class; required.
- Column: The name of the column to which it maps; required unless a formula is used.
- Length: For string or array properties, the maximum length of the column in the table. It is only used when generating the table or the column; not required an the default value is **255**.
- Not Null: Indicates if the properties' underlying column takes **NULL** values; must match the property type (for value types, if they might be nullable on the database, they must be declared with **?**); not required, the default is **false**.
- Formula: If set, it should be a SQL statement that may reference other columns of the entity's table; if set, the column property has no meaning.
- Unique: Indicates if the column should be unique; only used when the table or column is generated. Default is **false**.
- Optimistic Lock: If set to **false**, it won't consider this property for determining if the entity's version should change (more on versioning in the Optimistic chapter). It is not required and the default value is **true**.
- Update: Indicates if the column is considered for updating when the entity is updated; the default is **true**.
- Insert: If the column should be inserted or not; the default is **true**.
- Generated: If set, indicates if the column's value is generated upon insertion (**insert**) or **always**, generally by means of a trigger. The default is **never**, and if something else is used, an extra SELECT is needed after the insertion or update of the entity to know its value.
- Lazy: Should the column be loaded when the containing entity is loaded, we should set this to **true** if the column contains large contents (CLOBs or BLOBs) and its value may not always be required. The default is **false**.
- Type: If the property is not one of the primitive types, it should contain the full name of a concrete .NET class, which is responsible for creating the property's actual value from the column coming from the database and for translating it back into the database. There are several type implementations included with NHibernate.
- Mutable: Do changes to this property be reflected to the database? The default is **true**.

For scalar properties, either at entity level or as members of a component, NHibernate supports the following .NET types:

.NET Type	OOTB	Purpose
Boolean	Yes	A boolean or single bit (0/1 value)
Byte/SByte	Yes	8-bit signed/unsigned integer number, usually for representing a single ANSI character
Byte[]	Yes	Stored in a BLOB
Char	Yes	Single ANSI or UNICODE character
CultureInfo	Yes	Stored as a string containing the culture name
DateTime	Yes	Date and time
DateTimeOffset	Yes	Date and time with offset relative to UTC
Decimal	Yes	128-bit signed integers, scaled by a power of 10
Double	Yes	Double precision (64-bit) signed floating point values
Enum (enumerated type)	Yes/No	Stored as an integer (default), as a character or as a string
Guid	Yes	GUIDs or generic 128-bit numbers
Int16/UInt16	Yes	16-bit signed/unsigned integer numbers
Int32/UInt32	Yes	32-bit signed/unsigned integer numbers
Int64/UInt64	Yes	64-bit signed/unsigned integer numbers

.NET Type	OOTB	Purpose
Object (serializable)	No	Stored in a BLOB containing the object's contents after serialization
Single	Yes	Single precision (32-bit) signed floating point values
String	Yes	ANSI or UNICODE variable or fixed-length characters
TimeSpan	Yes	Time
Type	Yes	Stored as a string containing the assembly qualified type name
Uri	Yes	Stored as a string
XDocument/XmlDocument	Yes	XML

The second column indicates if the property's type is supported out of the box by NHibernate, that is, without the need for additional configuration. If we need to map a nonstandard primitive type or one of those other types that NHibernate recognizes out of the box (**Enum, DateTime, DateTimeOffset, Guid, TimeSpan, Uri, Type, CultureInfo, Byte[]**) or if we need to change the way a given property should be handled, we need to use a custom user type. For common cases, no type needs to be specified. For other scenarios, the available types are:

NHibernate Types

NHibernate Type	.NET Property Type	Description
AnsiCharType	**Char**	Stores a **Char** as an ANSI (8 bits per character) column instead of UNICODE (16 bits). Some national characters may be lost.
AnsiStringType	**String**	Stores a **String** as an ANSI (8 bits per character) column instead of UNICODE (16 bits). Some national characters may be lost.

NHibernate Type	.NET Property Type	Description
BinaryBlobType	Byte[]	Will store a **Byte[]** in a database-specific BLOB. If the database requires defining a maximum length, as in SQL Server, use **BinaryBlobType**.
CharBooleanType	Boolean	Converts a **Boolean** value to either **True** or **False**
DateType	DateTime	Stores only the date part of a **DateTime**
EnumCharType<T>	Enum (enumerated type)	Stores an enumerated value as a single character, obtained from its numeric value
EnumStringType<T>	Enum (enumerated type)	Stores an enumerated value as its string representation instead of its numeric value
LocalDateTimeType	DateTime	Stores a **DateTime** as local
SerializableType	Object (serializable)	Serializes an **Object** into a database-specific BLOB type.
StringClobType	String	Will store a **String** in a database-specific CLOB type instead of a standard VARCHAR
TicksType	DateTime	Stores a **DateTime** as a number of ticks
TrueFalseType	Boolean	Converts a **Boolean** value to either **T** or **F**
UtcDateTimeType	DateTime	Stores a **DateTime** as UTC
YesNoType	Boolean	Converts a **Boolean** value to either **Y** or **N**

Complex properties differ from references to other entities because all of their inner properties are stored in the same class as the declaring entity, and complex properties don't have anything like an identifier, just a collection of scalar properties. They are useful for logically grouping together some properties that conceptually are related (think of an address, for example). A component may be used in several classes and its only requirements are that it is not abstract and that it has a public, parameterless constructor.

A property does not have to be **public** but, at the least, it should be **protected**, not **private**. Its visibility will affect the ability of the querying APIs to use it; LINQ, for example, will only work with public properties. Different access levels for setters and getters are fine, too, as long as you keep them **protected** at most.

Finally, although you can use properties with an explicit backing field, there is really no need to do so. In fact, some functionality will not work with backing fields and, as a rule of thumb, you should stick to auto properties.

Custom Types

Some scenarios where we need to specify a type include, for example, when we need to store a **String** in a BLOB column such as **VARBINARY(MAX)** in SQL Server or when we need to store just the date part of a **DateTime** or even when we need to store a **Boolean** as its string representation (**True/False**). Like I said, in most cases, you do not need to worry about this.

You can create your own user type, for example, if you want to expose some columns as a different type—like converting a BLOB into an **Image**. See the following example:

```
[Serializable]
public sealed class ImageUserType : IUserType, IParameterizedType
{
    private Byte[] data = null;

    public ImageUserType() : this(ImageFormat.Png)
    {
    }

    public ImageUserType(ImageFormat imageFormat)
    {
        this.ImageFormat = imageFormat;
    }

    public ImageFormat ImageFormat { get; private set; }

    public override Int32 GetHashCode()
    {
        return ((this as IUserType).GetHashCode(this.data));
    }

    public override Boolean Equals(Object obj)
    {
        ImageUserType other = obj as ImageUserType;
```

```csharp
  if (other == null)
  {
    return (false);
  }

  if (Object.ReferenceEquals(this, other) == true)
  {
    return (true);
  }

  return (this.data.SequenceEqual(other.data));
}

Boolean IUserType.IsMutable
{
  get
  {
    return (true);
  }
}

Object IUserType.Assemble(Object cached, Object owner)
{
  return (cached);
}

Object IUserType.DeepCopy(Object value)
{
  if (value is ICloneable)
  {
    return ((value as ICloneable).Clone());
  }
  else
  {
    return (value);
  }
}

Object IUserType.Disassemble(Object value)
{
  return ((this as IUserType).DeepCopy(value));
}

Boolean IUserType.Equals(Object x, Object y)
{
  return (Object.Equals(x, y));
}

Int32 IUserType.GetHashCode(Object x)
{
  return ((x != null) ? x.GetHashCode() : 0);
}

Object IUserType.NullSafeGet(IDataReader rs, String[] names, Object owner)
{
  this.data = NHibernateUtil.Binary.NullSafeGet(rs, names) as Byte[];
```

```csharp
    if (data == null)
    {
      return (null);
    }

    using (Stream stream = new MemoryStream(this.data ?? new Byte[0]))
    {
      return (Image.FromStream(stream));
    }
  }

  void IUserType.NullSafeSet(IDbCommand cmd, Object value, Int32 index)
  {
    if (value != null)
    {
      Image data = value as Image;

      using (MemoryStream stream = new MemoryStream())
      {
        data.Save(stream, this.ImageFormat);
        value = stream.ToArray();
      }
    }

    NHibernateUtil.Binary.NullSafeSet(cmd, value, index);
  }

  Object IUserType.Replace(Object original, Object target, Object owner)
  {
    return (original);
  }

  Type IUserType.ReturnedType
  {
    get
    {
      return (typeof(Image));
    }
  }

  SqlType[] IUserType.SqlTypes
  {
    get
    {
      return (new SqlType[] { NHibernateUtil.BinaryBlob.SqlType });
    }
  }

void IParameterizedType.SetParameterValues(IDictionary<String, String> param
eters)
  {

if ((parameters != null) && (parameters.ContainsKey("ImageFormat") == true))
    {
```

```
this.ImageFormat = typeof(ImageFormat).GetProperty(parameters["ImageFormat"]
,
BindingFlags.Static | BindingFlags.Public | BindingFlags.GetProperty).GetVal
ue(null, null) as ImageFormat;
    }
  }
}
```

The most important aspects are:

- How the data is retrieved from and saved back to the data source (**NullSafeGet** and **NullSafeSet** methods)
- The value comparison, for letting NHibernate know if the property has changed (**Equals** and **GetHashCode**), for the purpose of change tracking
- The database data type (**SqlTypes**)

Identifiers

An identifier is either a scalar property, for the most general case of single column primary keys, or a custom class that contains properties for all the columns that make up the composite key. If it is a scalar property, not all types are allowed. You should only use primitive types (**Char**, **Byte/SByte**, **Int16/UInt16**, **Int32/UInt32**, **Int64/UInt64**, **Decimal**, **String**) and some specific value types (**Guid**, **DateTime**, **DateTimeOffset, TimeSpan**). BLOB, CLOB, and XML columns cannot be used as primary keys.

An identifier property may also be non-public but the most restricted access level you should use is **protected** or **protected internal**. Protected setters and public getters are fine, too, and are actually a good idea—unless you want to use manually assigned identifiers.

A very important concept around identifiers is the generation strategy. Basically, this is how the primary key is generated when a record is to be inserted into the database. These are the most important high-level strategies:

Strategy Type	Generator (by code/XML)	Identifier Property Type	Description
Database-generated	**Identity/identity** **Sequence/sequence**	**Int16/UInt16,** **Int32/UInt32,** **Int64/UInt64**	Identity columns are supported in SQL Server, MySQL, and Sybase, among others. Sequences are supported on Oracle and PostgreSQL, and can provide values for multiple tables. Both are safe for multiple simultaneous accesses but do not allow batching (more on this later).
GUID-based	**Guid/guid** **GuidComb/guid.comb**	**Guid**	GUIDs are generated by NHibernate and are assumed to be unique. It is safe for multiple simultaneous accesses and it is possible to do batch insertions. **GuidComb** is always sequencial.
Supported by a backing table	**HighLow/hilo**	**Int16/UInt16,** **Int32/UInt32,** **Int64/UInt64**	A table exists where the next high value is stored. When a session needs to insert records, it increments and updates this value and combines it with the next of a range of sequential low values until this range is exhausted and another high value needs to be retrieved. It is safe for both multiple simultaneous accesses and batching.
Manually assigned	**Assigned/assigned**	Any	You are responsible for assigning unique keys to your entities; use with care when you have multiple sessions inserting records.

There are other identifier generators but is advised that you stick with these because they are the ones supported by all mapping APIs. A discussion of these strategies is required.

Database-generated keys may be appealing because they are naturally used with common database programming and may appear as the natural choice. However, they do have some drawbacks:

- Because the key is generated inside the database after a record is inserted, an additional immediate SELECT is required to obtain the generated key. This renders batching impossible because we cannot issue multiple INSERTs together.
- Because both identity columns and sequences are designed for speed, they do not take into consideration database transactions. This means that, even if you rollback, the generated key, although not used, will be lost.
- They do not comply with the concept of Unit of Work, in the sense that it will try to insert the new record as soon as the entity is marked for saving and not just when the Unit of Work is committed.
- Most important: They are not database-independent. If you wish to use identity columns or sequences, you can only do it in engines that support this functionality, without changing the mapping configuration.

> 💡 *Tip: When using the* Sequence *generator, you have to supply the name for the actual sequence to be used as a parameter to the generator (see below).*

GUIDs have some interesting aspects:

- Because they are guaranteed to be unique, they are the obvious choice when it comes to designing a database that will be populated with records coming from third-party databases; there will never be clashes.
- They are fast to compute.
- They are database-independent.

They have one serious disadvantage, though: If we use clustered primary keys (the default in SQL Server), because generated GUIDs are not sequential they will make the engine continually reorganize the index, adding new keys either before or after the existing ones. To deal with this problem, NHibernate has implemented an alternative version, **GuidComb**, which is based on an algorithm designed by Jimmy Nilsson and available at http://www.informit.com/articles/article.aspx?p=25862. It basically consists of making a GUID sequential: two GUIDs generated in sequence are also numerically sequential, while remaining unique. If you really need a GUID as your primary key, do choose **GuidComb**. However, do keep in mind that GUIDs do take much more space—16 bytes as opposed to the four bytes of an integer.

The **HighLow** generation strategy is recommended for most scenarios. It is database-independent, allows batching, copes well with the Unit of Work concept, and, although it does require a SELECT and an UPDATE when the first record is to be inserted and additional ones when the low values are exhausted, the low values are immediately available. Plus, a range can be quite large, allowing for many records to be inserted without performing additional queries.

As for manually assigned identifiers, there are certainly scenarios where they are useful. But they have a big problem. Because NHibernate uses the identifier value (or lack thereof) to tell if a record is to be updated or inserted, it needs to issue a SELECT before persisting an entity in order to know if the record already exists. This defeats batching and may present problems if multiple sessions are to be used simultaneously.

Apart from the generation strategy, an identifier also supports the following properties:

- Name: The name of the .NET entity property; required.
- Column(s): The name of the column(s) that contain(s) the primary key; required.
- Length: For string columns, will contain their size, only for the purpose of generating the table or column. If not set, it defaults to **255**.
- Unsaved Value: A textual representation of the value that the identifier property has before the identifier is generated; used for distinguishing if the entity is new or updated. If not set, it defaults to the identifier property's underlying default value (**0** for numbers, **null** for classes, etc).

It is possible to pass parameters to identifier generators for those that require it. One example would be specifying the sequence name for the **Sequence** generator. Examples are included in the mapping sections.

References

Like table relations, an entity may also be associated with another entity. It is said that the entity's class has a reference for another entity's class. There are two types of relations:

- **One-to-one**: The primary key is shared between the two tables. For each record on the main table, there may be, at most, one record on the secondary table that refers to it. Useful when you have mandatory data and optional data that is associated with it.
- **Many-to-one**: A table's record may be associated with one record from another table. This other record may be referenced by multiple records on the main table. Think of it as a record's parent.

A reference has the type of the class on the other endpoint. There can be even multiple references to the same class, of course, with different names. The properties of the reference are:

- Name: Mandatory.
- Required: If the record on the main class must reference an existing record on the second class. The default is **false**.
- The relation type: Either **one-to-one** or **many-to-one**.
- Laziness: The default is **proxy**, meaning that the referenced entity will not be loaded at the same time as its referencing entity but, rather, a proxy will be created for it (which will cause it to load when accessed). Other possibilities are **false** or **no-proxy**.
- Not found: The behavior when the referenced record is not found. The default is **exception** and the other possibility is **ignore**.

Collections

An entity (parent) can be associated with multiple entities (children) of some type at the same time. These collections can be characterized in a number of ways:

- Endpoint multiplicity: One-to-many (a parent has multiple children, a child only has one parent), many-to-many (a parent can have multiple children and each child can have multiple parents), and values (the children are not entities but values).
- Relation between the parent and the children endpoints: Unidirectional (the parent knows the children but these do not know the parent), and bidirectional (both sides know each other).
- Conceptually: Bag (allows duplicates, order does not matter), and set (does not allow duplicates, elements are either sorted or unsorted).
- What they contain: Values (scalar values), components (complex values without an identity of their own), and entities (complex values with their own identity).
- How they are accessed: Indexed or keyed (something is used for identifying each of the items in the collection) and non-indexed.
- Where is the foreign key stored: Inverse (the foreign key is located at the child endpoint) or non-inverse.

NHibernate has the following collection types:

NHibernate Collection Types

Collection	Relations	Items to Store	Index Type	.NET Types
Set (non-indexed, bidirectional, inverse)	One-to-many, many-to-many	Entities, elements, components	N/A	**IEnumerable<T>, ICollection<T>, Iesi.Collections.Generic.ISet<T>**
Bag (non-indexed, bidirectional, inverse or non-inverse)	One-to-many, many-to-many, values	Entities, values, components	N/A	**IEnumerable<T>, ICollection<T>, IList<T>**
List (indexed, bidirectional, inverse or non-inverse)	One-to-many, many-to-many, values	Entities, values, components	Number	**IEnumerable<T>, ICollection<T>, IList<T>**
Map (indexed, unidirectional, inverse or non-inverse)	Many-to-many, values	Entities, values, components	Entity, scalar value	**IDictionary<TKey, TValue>**

Collection	Relations	Items to Store	Index Type	.NET Types
Id Bag (non-indexed, unidirectional, inverse or non-inverse)	One-to-many, Many-to-many, values	Entities, values, components	Number	**IEnumerable<T>, ICollection<T>, IList<T>**
Array (indexed, unidirectional, inverse or non-inverse)	One-to-many, many-to-many, values	Entities, values, components	Number	**IEnumerable<T>, ICollection<T>, T []**
Primitive Array (indexed, unidirectional, non-inverse)	One-to-many, many-to-many, values	Values of primitive types	Number	**IEnumerable<T>, ICollection<T>, T []**

 Tip: You cannot use the .NET BCL System.Collections.Generic.ISet<T>; **as of now, NHibernate requires the use of** lesi.Collections.

Collections have the following attributes:

- Name: This is mandatory.
- Type (**bag, set, list, map, id bag, array, primitive array**): This is also mandatory.
- Key: The name of the column or entity (in the case of **maps**) that contains the key of the relation.
- Order: The column by which the collection's elements will be loaded. Optional.
- Whether the collection is **inverse** or not (**set, list, id bag, array, primitive array**): Default is **false**.
- The entity or element type of its values: Mandatory.
- Restriction: An optional restriction SQL (see Restrictions).
- Laziness: The desired laziness of the collection (see Lazy Loading). The default is **lazy**.
- Endpoint Multiplicity: One-to-many or many-to-many in the case of collections of entities. Mandatory.

Some remarks:

- NHibernate fully supports generic collections and you really should use them.
- All except **array** and **primitive array** support lazy loading. **Arrays** and **primitive arrays** cannot change their size; that is, it is not possible to add or remove items.
- The .NET type you use to declare the collection should always be an interface. The actual type will determine what you want to be able to do with the collection. For

example, **IEnumerable<T>** does not allow modifications, which makes it a good choice for scenarios in which you don't want users to change the content of the collection.

- All collection types other than **primitive array** support entities, primitive types, and components as their items.
- **Id bags**, **lists**, **arrays**, and **primitive arrays** use an additional table column, not mapped to a class property, to store the primary key (in the case of **id bags**) or the ordering. If you use NHibernate to create the data model, NHibernate will create it for you.
- Bidirectional relations between entities are always **inverse**.
- Maps, collections of components (complex properties), elements (primitive types), and **primitive arrays** are never **inverse**.
- Maps and many-to-many relations always require an additional mapping table.
- By far, the most often used collections are **sets**, **lists**, and **maps**.
- When compared to **bags**, **sets** have the advantage in that they do not allow duplicates which, most of the time, is what we want.
- Because **bags** do not know the key of their elements, whenever we add or remove from a **bag**, we need to remove and re-insert all elements, which leads to terrible performance. **Id bags** solve this problem by allowing an unmapped key column.
- **Lists** are better than **arrays** as indexed collections because **arrays** cannot change their size.
- **Maps** are great for indexing a collection by something other than a number.
- There should seldom be a need for **array** mappings.

Sets and bags are stored using only one table for each entity, and one of these tables contains a foreign key for the other:

Figure 12: Sets and Bags Class and Table Model

It will typically be declared like this in code:

```
public virtual Iesi.Collections.Generic.ISet<Comment> Comments { get;
protected set; }
```

Lists also need only two tables, but they use an additional, unmapped column for storing one entity's order in its parent's collection:

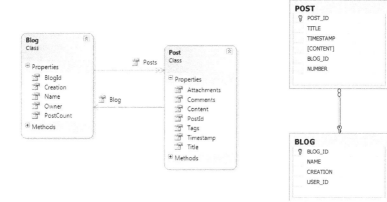

Figure 13: One-to-Many/Many-to-One Class and Table Model

A **list** (and also a **bag**) is mapped as an **IList<T>** and the order of its elements is dictated by the **list**'s indexed column attribute, which must be an integer.

```
public virtual IList<Post> Posts { get; protected set; }
```

Many-to-many relations do require an additional mapping table, which does not translate to any class but is used transparently by NHibernate:

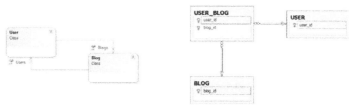

Figure 14: Many-to-Many Class and Table Model

These are represented by two **set** collections, one on each class, only one of them being **inverse**.

```
public class User
{
    public virtual Iesi.Collections.Generic.ISet<Blog> Blogs { get;
protected set; }
}
```

```
public class Blog
{
  public virtual Iesi.Collections.Generic.ISet<User> Users { get;
protected set; }
}
```

Maps also need an additional table for storing the additional property (in the case where the value is a single scalar) or the key to the other endpoint entity (for a one-to-many relation):

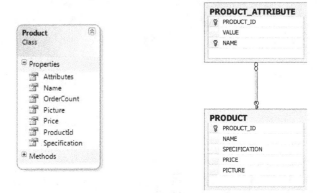

Figure 15: Map Class and Table Model

Maps are represented in .NET by **IDictionary<TKey, TValue>**. The key is always the containing class and the values can either be entities (in which we have a one-to-many or many-to-many relation), components (complex properties) or elements (primitive types).

```
public virtual IDictionary<String, String> Attributes { get; protected set;
}
```

XML Mappings

Now we get to the bottom of it all. In the beginning, NHibernate only had XML-based mappings. This is still supported and it basically means that, for every entity, there must be a corresponding XML file that describes how the class binds to the data model (you can have a single file for all mappings but this makes it more difficult to find a specific mapping). The XML file must bind the entity class to a database table and declare the properties and associations that it will recognize. One important property that must be present is the one that contains the identifier for the entity instance, the table's primary key.

By convention, NHibernate's XML mapping files end with **HBM.XML** (in any case). The mappings for this example might be (bear with me, an explanation follows shortly):

The way to add IntelliSense to the **HBM.XML** files is like this:

1. Download the XML Schema Definition (XSD) file for the configuration section from https://github.com/nhibernate/nhibernate-core/blob/master/src/NHibernate/nhibernate-mapping.xsd.
2. Open the **.HBM.XML** file where you have a mapping configuration in Visual Studio.
3. Go to the **Properties** window and select the ellipsis (…) button next to **Schemas**.
4. Click the **Add…** button and select the **nhibernate-mapping.xsd** file that you just downloaded.
5. Select **Use this Schema** at the line with target namespace **urn:nhibernate-mapping-2.2**.

First, the mapping for the **User** class, which should go in a **User.hbm.xml** file:

```
<?xml version="1.0" encoding="utf-8"?>
<hibernate-
mapping namespace="Succinctly.Model" assembly="Succinctly.Model" xmlns="urn:
nhibernate-mapping-2.2">
  <class name="User" lazy="true" table="`user`">
    <id name="UserId" column="`user_id`" generator="hilo" />
    <property name="Username" column="`username`" length="10" not-
null="true" />
    <property name="Birthday" column="`birthday`" not-null="false" />
    <component name="Details">
      <property name="Fullname" column="`fullname`" length="50" not-
null="true" />
      <property name="Email" column="`email`" length="50" not-null="true" />
      <property name="Url" column="`url`" length="50" not-null="false" />
    </component>
    <set cascade="all-delete-
orphan" inverse="true" lazy="true" name="Blogs">
      <key column="`user_id`" />
      <one-to-many class="Blog" />
    </set>
  </class>
</hibernate-mapping>
```

Next, the **Blog** class (**Blog.hbm.xml**):

```
<?xml version="1.0" encoding="utf-8"?>
<hibernate-
mapping namespace="Succinctly.Model" assembly="Succinctly.Model" xmlns="urn:
nhibernate-mapping-2.2">
  <class name="Blog" lazy="true" table="`blog`">
    <id name="BlogId" column="`blog_id `" generator="hilo" />
    <property name="Name" column="`NAME`" length="50" not-null="true" />
    <property name="Creation" column="`creation`" not-null="true" />
    <property name="PostCount"
formula="(SELECT COUNT(1) FROM post WHERE post.blog_id = blog_id)" />
    <property name="Picture" column="`PICTURE`" not-
null="false" lazy="true">
      <type name="Succinctly.Common.ImageUserType, Succinctly.Common"/>
    </property>
    <many-to-one name="Owner" column="`user_id`" not-null="true" lazy="no-
proxy" cascade="save-update"/>
    <list cascade="all-delete-
orphan" inverse="true" lazy="true" name="Posts">
```

```
        <key column="`blog_id`" />
        <index column="`number`" />
        <one-to-many class="Post" />
    </list>
  </class>
</hibernate-mapping>
```

The **Post** (**Post.hbm.xml**):

```
<?xml version="1.0" encoding="utf-8"?>
<hibernate-
mapping namespace="Succinctly.Model" assembly="Succinctly.Model" xmlns="urn:
nhibernate-mapping-2.2">
  <class name="Post" lazy="true" table="`post`">
    <id name="PostId" column="`post_id`" generator="hilo" />
    <property name="Title" column="`title`" length="50" not-null="true" />
    <property name="Timestamp" column="`timestamp`" not-null="true" />

<property name="Content" type="StringClob" column="`content`" length="2000"
not-null="true" lazy="true" />
    <many-to-one name="Blog" column="`blog_id`" not-null="true" lazy="no-
proxy" />
    <set cascade="all" lazy="true" name="Tags" table="`tag`" order-
by="`tag`">
      <key column="`post_id`" />
      <element column="`tag`" type="String" length="20" not-
null="true" unique="true" />
    </set>
    <set cascade="all-delete-
orphan" inverse="true" lazy="true" name="Attachments">
      <key column="`post_id`" />
      <one-to-many class="Attachment" />
    </set>
    <bag cascade="all-delete-
orphan" inverse="true" lazy="true" name="Comments">
      <key column="`post_id`" />
      <one-to-many class="Comment" />
    </bag>
  </class>
</hibernate-mapping>
```

A **Post**'s **Comments** (**Comment.hbm.xml**):

```
<?xml version="1.0" encoding="utf-8"?>
<hibernate-
mapping namespace="Succinctly.Model" assembly="Succinctly.Model" xmlns="urn:
nhibernate-mapping-2.2">
  <class name="Comment" lazy="true" table="`comment`">
    <id name="CommentId" column="`comment_id`" generator="hilo" />
    <property name="Timestamp" column="`timestamp`" not-null="true" />

<property name="Content" type="StringClob" column="`content`" length="2000"
not-null="true" lazy="true" />
    <component name="Details">
```

```
        <property name="Fullname" column="`fullname`" length="50" not-
null="true" />
        <property name="Email" column="`email`" length="50" not-null="true" />
        <property name="Url" column="`url`" length="50" not-null="false" />
    </component>
        <many-to-one name="Post" column="`post_id`" not-null="true" lazy="no-
proxy" />
    </class>
</hibernate-mapping>
```

And, finally, a **Post**'s **Attachments** (**Attachment.hbm.xml**):

```
<?xml version="1.0" encoding="utf-8"?>
<hibernate-
mapping namespace="Succinctly.Model" assembly="Succinctly.Model" xmlns="urn:
nhibernate-mapping-2.2">
    <class name="Attachment" lazy="true" table="`attachment`">
        <id name="AttachmentId" column="`attachment_id`" generator="hilo" />
        <property name="Filename" column="`filename`" length="50" not-
null="true" />
        <property name="Timestamp" column="`timestamp`" not-null="true" />

<property name="Contents" type="BinaryBlob" column="`contents`" length="1000
00" not-null="true" lazy="true" />
        <many-to-one name="Post" column="`post_id`" not-null="true" lazy="no-
proxy" />
    </class>
</hibernate-mapping>
```

Let's analyze what we have here.

First, all entities have a **class** mapping declaration. On this declaration we have:

- The class **name**
- The **table** name where the entity is to be persisted
- The desired laziness; always **lazy** in this example

Next, we always need an identifier declaration. In it, we have the following attributes:

- The property **name** that contains the identifier
- The **column** name that contains the identifier

The **generator** strategy or class (in our examples, always **hilo**), see section The most important aspects are:

- How the data is retrieved from and saved back to the data source (**NullSafeGet** and **NullSafeSet** methods)
- The value comparison, for letting NHibernate know if the property has changed (**Equals** and **GetHashCode**), for the purpose of change tracking
- The database data type (**SqlTypes**)
- Identifiers

If we need to pass parameters, we can do it like this:

```
<?xml version="1.0" encoding="utf-8"?>
<hibernate-
mapping namespace="Succinctly.Model" assembly="Succinctly.Model" xmlns="urn:
nhibernate-mapping-2.2">
  <class name="Attachment" lazy="true" table="`attachment`">
    <id name="AttachmentId" column="`attachment_id`" generator="hilo">
      <param name="sequence">ATTACHMENT_SEQUENCE</param>
    </id>
  <!-- … -->
</hibernate-mapping>
```

Then, we have scalar property declarations. For each property we need:

- The property **name**.
- The **column** name.
- If the column needs to be **not-null**.
- The desired **lazy** setting.
- Optionally, a SQL formula, in which case the column name will not be used (see the **PostCount** property of the **Blog** class).
- The length of the column, for strings only.
- In some cases, we have a **type** declaration (**Post.Content**, **Blog.Picture** properties). The **Blog.Picture** property references by assembly qualified name a custom user type (**ImageUserType**). This user type allows translating a BLOB column (**Byte[]**) to a .NET **Image**, which can be very handy.

We have some complex properties for which we use component declarations. They are useful for storing values that conceptually should be together (see the mappings for the **Details** property of the **User** class and the **Details** property of the **Comment** class). A component contains:

- The property **name**.
- Optionally, a **lazy** declaration.
- One or more scalar property mappings (**column**, **length**, **not-null**).

References come up next. With it, we declare that our entities are associated to the children of another entity. See, for example, the **Blog** association of the **Post** entity. A typical mapping includes:

- The property **name**.
- The **column** name that stores the foreign key.
- Indication if the foreign key can be **not-null**, for optional references.
- The desired **lazy** option.

Finally, we have collections. These can be of several types (for a discussion, see the Collections section). In this example, we have collections of entities (for example, see the **Comments** collection of the **Post** entity) and collections of strings (the **Tags** collections of the **Post** class, mapped as **bags**, **lists** and **sets**, respectively). The possible attributes depend on the actual collection but all include:

- The property **name**.
- The kind of collection (**list**, **set** or **bag**, in this example).

- The **lazy** option.
- The column that contains the foreign **key**, which should generally match the primary key of the main entity.
- The **index** column, in the case of **lists**.
- The entity **class** that represents the child side of the one-to-many relation (for collections of entities).
- The value's **type**, **length**, **column**, and **unique**ness (for collections of scalar values).

If you are to use mapping by XML, pay attention to this: You can either include the **HBM.XML** files as embedded resources in the assembly where the classes live or you can have them as external files.

If you want to include the resource files as embedded resources, which is probably a good idea because you have less files to deploy, make sure of two things:

- The project that includes the entity classes should have a base namespace that is identical to the base namespace of these classes (say, for example, **Succinctly.Model**):

Figure 16: Setting Project Properties

- The **HBM.XML** files should be located in the same folder as the classes to which they refer.
- Each **HBM.XML** file should be marked as an embedded resource:

Figure 17: Setting Embedded Resources

- For loading mappings from embedded resources, use the **AddAssembly** method of the **Configuration** instance or the **<mapping assembly>** tag in case in XML configuration:

```
//add an assembly by name
cfg.AddAssembly("Succinctly.Model");
//add an Assembly instance
cfg.AddAssembly(typeof(Blog).Assembly);
```

```
<session-factory>
  <!-- … -->
  <mapping assembly="Succinctly.Model" />
</session-factory>
```

 Tip: Beware! Any changes you make to HBM.XML files are not automatically detected by Visual Studio so you will have to build the project explicitly whenever you change anything.

If you prefer instead to have external files:

```
//add a single file
cfg.AddFile("Blog.hbm.xml");
//add all .HBM.XML files in a directory
cfg.AddDirectory(new DirectoryInfo("."));
```

Mapping by Code

Mapping by code is new in NHibernate as of version 3.2. Its advantage is that there is no need for additional mapping files and, because it is strongly typed, it is more refactor-friendly. For example, if you change the name of a property, the mapping will reflect that change immediately.

With mapping by code, you typically add a new class for each entity that you wish to map and have that class inherit from **NHibernate.Mapping.ByCode.Conformist.ClassMapping<T>** where **T** is the entity class. The following code will result in the exact same mapping as the **HBM.XML** version. You can see that there are similarities in the code structure and the method names closely resemble the XML tags.

UserMapping class:

```
public class UserMapping : ClassMapping<User>
{
  public UserMapping()
  {
    this.Table("user");
    this.Lazy(true);
```

```
    this.Id(x => x.UserId, x =>
    {
      x.Column("user_id");
      x.Generator(Generators.HighLow);
    });

    this.Property(x => x.Username, x =>
    {
      x.Column("username");
      x.Length(20);
      x.NotNullable(true);
    });
    this.Property(x => x.Birthday, x =>
    {
      x.Column("birthday");
      x.NotNullable(false);
    });
    this.Component(x => x.Details, x =>
    {
      x.Property(y => y.Fullname, z =>
      {
        z.Column("fullname");
        z.Length(50);
        z.NotNullable(true);
      });
      x.Property(y => y.Email, z =>
      {
        z.Column("email");
        z.Length(50);
        z.NotNullable(true);
      });
      x.Property(y => y.Url, z =>
      {
        z.Column("url");
        z.Length(50);
        z.NotNullable(false);
      });
    });

    this.Set(x => x.Blogs, x =>
    {
      x.Key(y =>
      {
        y.Column("user_id");
        y.NotNullable(true);
      });
      x.Cascade(Cascade.All | Cascade.DeleteOrphans);
      x.Inverse(true);
      x.Lazy(CollectionLazy.Lazy);
    }, x =>
    {
      x.OneToMany();
    });
  }
}
```

💡 *Tip: **Add a using statement for namespaces** NHibernate,*
*NHibernate.Mapping.ByCode.Conformist, NHibernate.Mapping.ByCode, **and***
NHibernate.Type.

BlogMapping class:

```
public class BlogMapping : ClassMapping<Blog>
{
  public BlogMapping()
  {
    this.Table("blog");
    this.Lazy(true);

    this.Id(x => x.BlogId, x =>
    {
      x.Column("blog_id");
      x.Generator(Generators.HighLow);
    });

    this.Property(x => x.Name, x =>
    {
      x.Column("name");
      x.Length(50);
      x.NotNullable(true);
    });
    this.Property(x => x.Picture, x =>
    {
      x.Column("picture");
      x.NotNullable(false);
      x.Type<ImageUserType>();
      x.Lazy(true);
    });
    this.Property(x => x.Creation, x =>
    {
      x.Column("creation");
      x.NotNullable(true);
    });
    this.Property(x => x.PostCount, x =>
    {
      x.Formula("(SELECT COUNT(1) FROM post WHERE post.blog_id = blog_id)");
    });

    this.ManyToOne(x => x.Owner, x =>
    {
      x.Cascade(Cascade.Persist);
      x.Column("user_id");
      x.NotNullable(true);
      x.Lazy(LazyRelation.NoProxy);
    });

    this.List(x => x.Posts, x =>
    {
      x.Key(y =>
      {
```

```
      y.Column("blog_id");
      y.NotNullable(true);
    });
    x.Index(y =>
    {
      y.Column("number");
    });
    x.Lazy(CollectionLazy.Lazy);
    x.Cascade(Cascade.All | Cascade.DeleteOrphans);
    x.Inverse(true);
  }, x =>
  {
    x.OneToMany();
  });
  }
}
```

PostMapping class:

```
public class PostMapping : ClassMapping<Post>
  {
    public PostMapping()
    {
      this.Table("post");
      this.Lazy(true);

      this.Id(x => x.PostId, x =>
      {
        x.Column("post_id");
        x.Generator(Generators.HighLow);
      });

      this.Property(x => x.Title, x =>
      {
        x.Column("title");
        x.Length(50);
        x.NotNullable(true);
      });
      this.Property(x => x.Timestamp, x =>
      {
        x.Column("timestamp");
        x.NotNullable(true);
      });
      this.Property(x => x.Content, x =>
      {
        x.Column("content");
        x.Length(2000);
        x.NotNullable(true);
        x.Type(NHibernateUtil.StringClob);
      });

      this.ManyToOne(x => x.Blog, x =>
      {
        x.Column("blog_id");
        x.NotNullable(true);
        x.Lazy(LazyRelation.NoProxy);
```

```
    });

    this.Set(x => x.Tags, x =>
    {
      x.Key(y =>
      {
        y.Column("post_id");
        y.NotNullable(true);
      });
      x.Cascade(Cascade.All);
      x.Lazy(CollectionLazy.NoLazy);
      x.Fetch(CollectionFetchMode.Join);
      x.Table("tag");
    }, x =>
    {
      x.Element(y =>
      {
        y.Column("tag");
        y.Length(20);
        y.NotNullable(true);
        y.Unique(true);
      });
    });
    this.Set(x => x.Attachments, x =>
    {
      x.Key(y =>
      {
        y.Column("post_id");
        y.NotNullable(true);
      });
      x.Cascade(Cascade.All | Cascade.DeleteOrphans);
      x.Lazy(CollectionLazy.Lazy);
      x.Inverse(true);
    }, x =>
    {
      x.OneToMany();
    });
    this.Bag(x => x.Comments, x =>
    {
      x.Key(y =>
      {
        y.Column("post_id");
      });
      x.Cascade(Cascade.All | Cascade.DeleteOrphans);
      x.Lazy(CollectionLazy.Lazy);
      x.Inverse(true);
    }, x =>
    {
      x.OneToMany();
    });
  }
}
```

CommentMapping class:

```
public class CommentMapping : ClassMapping<Comment>
```

```csharp
{
  public CommentMapping()
  {
    this.Table("comment");
    this.Lazy(true);

    this.Id(x => x.CommentId, x =>
    {
      x.Column("comment_id");
      x.Generator(Generators.HighLow);
    });

    this.Property(x => x.Content, x =>
    {
      x.Column("content");
      x.NotNullable(true);
      x.Length(2000);
      x.Lazy(true);
      x.Type(NHibernateUtil.StringClob);
    });
    this.Property(x => x.Timestamp, x =>
    {
      x.Column("timestamp");
      x.NotNullable(true);
    });

    this.Component(x => x.Details, x =>
    {
      x.Property(y => y.Fullname, z =>
      {
        z.Column("fullname");
        z.Length(50);
        z.NotNullable(true);
      });
      x.Property(y => y.Email, z =>
      {
        z.Column("email");
        z.Length(50);
        z.NotNullable(true);
      });
      x.Property(y => y.Url, z =>
      {
        z.Column("url");
        z.Length(50);
        z.NotNullable(false);
      });
    });

    this.ManyToOne(x => x.Post, x =>
    {
      x.Column("post_id");
      x.NotNullable(true);
      x.Lazy(LazyRelation.NoProxy);
    });
  }
}
```

AttachmentMapping class:

```
public class AttachmentMapping : ClassMapping<Attachment>
{
  public AttachmentMapping()
  {
    this.Table("attachment");
    this.Lazy(true);

    this.Id(x => x.AttachmentId, x =>
    {
      x.Column("attachment_id");
      x.Generator(Generators.HighLow);
    });

    this.Property(x => x.Filename, x =>
    {
      x.Column("filename");
      x.Length(50);
      x.NotNullable(true);
    });
    this.Property(x => x.Timestamp, x =>
    {
      x.Column("timestamp");
      x.NotNullable(true);
    });
    this.Property(x => x.Contents, x =>
    {
      x.Column("contents");
      x.Length(100000);
      x.Type<BinaryBlobType>();
      x.NotNullable(true);
      x.Lazy(true);
    });

    this.ManyToOne(x => x.Post, x =>
    {
      x.Column("post_id");
      x.Lazy(LazyRelation.NoProxy);
      x.NotNullable(true);
    });
  }
}
```

Notice that for every thing (but table and columns names and raw SQL) there are strongly typed options and enumerations. All options are pretty similar to their **HBM.XML** counterpart, so moving from one mapping to the other should be straightforward.

For passing parameters to the generator, one would use the following method:

```
public class AttachmentMapping : ClassMapping<Attachment>
{
  public AttachmentMapping()
  {
    this.Table("attachment");
```

```
    this.Lazy(true);

    this.Id(x => x.AttachmentId, x =>
    {
      x.Column("attachment_id");

x.Generator(Generators.HighLow, x => x.Params(new { sequence = "ATTACHMENT_S
EQUENCE" } ));
    });
    //…
}
```

One problem with mapping by code—or more generally speaking, with LINQ expressions—is that you can only access **public** members. However, NHibernate lets you access both public as well as non-public members. If you want to map non-public classes, you have to use their names, for example:

```
this.Id("AttachmentId", x =>
{
  //…
});

this.Property("Filename", x =>
{
  //…
});

this.ManyToOne("Post", x =>
{
  //…
});
```

Now that you have mapping classes, you need to tie them to the **Configuration** instance. Three ways to do this:

1. One class mapping at a time (instance of **ClassMapping<T>**)
2. A static array of mappings
3. A dynamically obtained array

```
Configuration cfg = BuildConfiguration(); //whatever way you like
ModelMapper mapper = new ModelMapper();

//1: one class at a time
mapper.AddMapping<BlogMapping>();
mapper.AddMapping<UserMapping>();
mapper.AddMapping<PostMapping>();
mapper.AddMapping<CommentMapping>();
mapper.AddMapping<AttachmentMapping>();

//2: or all at once (pick one or the other, not both)
mapper.AddMappings(new Type[] { typeof(BlogMapping), typeof(UserMapping), ty
peof(PostMapping),
typeof(CommentMapping), typeof(AttachmentMapping) });

//3: or even dynamically found types (pick one or the other, not both)
```

```
mapper.AddMappings(typeof(BlogMapping).Assembly.GetTypes().Where(x => x.Base
Type.IsGenericType && x.BaseType.GetGenericTypeDefinition() == typeof(ClassM
apping<>)));

//code to be executed in all cases.
HbmMapping mappings = mapper.CompileMappingForAllExplicitlyAddedEntities();
cfg.AddDeserializedMapping(mappings, null);
```

For completeness' sake, let me tell you that you can use mapping by code without creating a class for each entity to map by using the methods in the **ModelMapper** class:

```
mapper.Class<Blog>(ca =>
{
  ca.Table("blog");
  ca.Lazy(true);
  ca.Id(x => x.BlogId, map =>
  {
    map.Column("blog_id");
    map.Generator(Generators.HighLow);
  });

  //...
```

I won't include a full mapping here but I think you get the picture. All calls should be identical to what you would have inside a **ClassMapping<T>**.

Mapping by Attributes

Yet another option is mapping by attributes. With this approach, you decorate your entity classes and properties with attributes that describe how they are mapped to database objects. The advantage with this is that your mapping becomes self-described, but you must add and deploy a reference to the **NHibernate.Mapping.Attributes** assembly, which is something that POCO purists may not like.

First, you must add a reference to NHibernate.Mapping.Attributes either by NuGet or by downloading the binaries from the SourceForge site at http://sourceforge.net/projects/nhcontrib/files/NHibernate.Mapping.Attributes. Let's choose NuGet:

```
PM> Install-Package NHibernate.Mapping.Attributes
```

Make sure that the project that contains your entities references the **NHibernate.Mapping.Attributes** assembly. After that, make the following changes to your entities, after adding a reference to **NHibernate.Mapping.Attributes** namespace:

User class:

```
[Class(Table = "user", Lazy = true)]
public class User
{
  public User()
  {
    this.Blogs = new Iesi.Collections.Generic.HashedSet<Blog>();
    this.Details = new UserDetail();
  }

  [Id(0, Column = "user_id", Name = "UserId")]
  [Generator(1, Class = "hilo")]
  public virtual Int32 UserId { get; protected set; }

  [Property(Name = "Username",
Column = "username", Length = 20, NotNull = true)]
  public virtual String Username { get; set; }

  [ComponentProperty(PropertyName = "Details")]
  public virtual UserDetail Details { get; set; }

  [Property(Name = "Birthday", Column = "birthday", NotNull = false)]
  public virtual DateTime? Birthday { get; set; }

  [Set(0, Name = "Blogs", Cascade = "all-delete-
orphan", Lazy = CollectionLazy.True, Inverse = true,
Generic = true)]
  [Key(1, Column = "user_id", NotNull = true)]
  [OneToMany(2, ClassType = typeof(Blog))]
  public virtual Iesi.Collections.Generic.ISet<Blog> Blogs { get;
protected set; }
}
```

Blog class:

```
[Class(Table = "blog", Lazy = true)]
public class Blog
{
  public Blog()
  {
    this.Posts = new List<Post>();
  }

  [Id(0, Column = "blog_id", Name = "BlogId")]
  [Generator(1, Class = "hilo")]
  public virtual Int32 BlogId { get; protected set; }


[Property(Column = "picture", NotNull = false, TypeType = typeof(ImageUserTy
pe), Lazy = true)]
  public virtual Image Picture { get; set; }

  [Property(Name = "PostCount",
Formula = "(SELECT COUNT(1) FROM post WHERE post.blog_id = blog_id)")]
  public virtual Int64 PostCount { get; protected set; }
```

```
[ManyToOne(0, Column = "user_id", NotNull = true, Lazy = Laziness.NoProxy, N
ame = "Owner",
Cascade = "save-update")]
  [Key(1)]
  public virtual User Owner { get; set; }

  [Property(Name = "Name", Column = "name", NotNull = true, Length = 50)]
  public virtual String Name { get; set; }

  [Property(Name = "Creation", Column = "creation", NotNull = true)]
  public virtual DateTime Creation { get; set; }

  [List(0, Name = "Posts", Cascade = "all-delete-
orphan", Lazy = CollectionLazy.True, Inverse = true,
Generic = true)]
  [Key(1, Column = "blog_id", NotNull = true)]
  [Index(2, Column = "number")]
  [OneToMany(3, ClassType = typeof(Post))]
  public virtual IList<Post> Posts { get; protected set; }
}
```

Post class:

```
[Class(Table = "post", Lazy = true)]
public class Post
{
  public Post()
  {
    this.Tags = new Iesi.Collections.Generic.HashedSet<String>();
    this.Attachments = new Iesi.Collections.Generic.HashedSet<Attachment>();
    this.Comments = new List<Comment>();
  }

  [Id(0, Column = "post_id", Name = "PostId")]
  [Generator(1, Class = "hilo")]
  public virtual Int32 PostId { get; protected set; }


[ManyToOne(0, Column = "blog_id", NotNull = true, Lazy = Laziness.NoProxy, N
ame = "Blog")]
  [Key(1)]
  public virtual Blog Blog { get; set; }

  [Property(Name = "Timestamp", Column = "timestamp", NotNull = true)]
  public virtual DateTime Timestamp { get; set; }

  [Property(Name = "Title", Column = "title", Length = 50, NotNull = true)]
  public virtual String Title { get; set; }

  [Property(Name = "Content",
Column = "content", Length = 2000, NotNull = true, Lazy = true,
Type = "StringClob")]
  public virtual String Content { get; set; }
```

```
   [Set(0, Name = "Tags",
Table = "tag", OrderBy = "tag", Lazy = CollectionLazy.False,
Cascade = "all", Generic = true)]
   [Key(1, Column = "post_id", Unique = true, NotNull = true)]
   [Element(2, Column = "tag", Length = 20, NotNull = true, Unique = true)]
   public virtual Iesi.Collections.Generic.ISet<String> Tags { get;
protected set; }

   [Set(0, Name = "Attachments",
Inverse = true, Lazy = CollectionLazy.True, Generic = true,
Cascade = "all-delete-orphan")]
   [Key(1, Column = "post_id", NotNull = true)]
   [OneToMany(2, ClassType = typeof(Attachment))]
   public virtual Iesi.Collections.Generic.ISet<Attachment> Attachments {
get; protected set; }

   [Bag(0, Name = "Comments",
Inverse = true, Lazy = CollectionLazy.True, Generic = true,
Cascade = "all-delete-orphan")]
   [Key(1, Column = "post_id", NotNull = true)]
   [OneToMany(2, ClassType = typeof(Comment))]
   public virtual IList<Comment> Comments { get; protected set; }
}
```

Comment class:

```
[Class(Table = "comment", Lazy = true)]
public class Comment
{
   public Comment()
   {
     this.Details = new UserDetail();
   }

   [Id(0, Column = "comment_id", Name = "CommentId")]
   [Generator(1, Class = "hilo")]
   public virtual Int32 CommentId { get; protected set; }

   [ComponentProperty(PropertyName = "Details")]
   public virtual UserDetail Details { get; set; }

   [Property(Name = "Timestamp", Column = "timestamp", NotNull = true)]
   public virtual DateTime Timestamp { get; set; }

   [Property(Name = "Content",
Column = "content", NotNull = true, Length = 2000, Lazy = true,
Type = "StringClob")]
   public virtual String Content { get; set; }


[ManyToOne(0, Column = "post_id", NotNull = true, Lazy = Laziness.NoProxy, N
ame = "Post")]
   [Key(1)]
   public virtual Post Post { get; set; }
}
```

Attachment class:

```
[Class(Table = "attachment", Lazy = true)]
public class Attachment
{
  [Id(0, Column = "attachment_id", Name = "AttachmentId")]
  [Generator(1, Class = "hilo")]
  public virtual Int32 AttachmentId { get; protected set; }

  [Property(Name = "Filename",
Column = "filename", Length = 50, NotNull = true)]
  public virtual String Filename { get; set; }

  [Property(Name = "Contents",
Column = "contents", NotNull = true, Length = 100000,
Type = "BinaryBlob")]
  public virtual Byte[] Contents { get; set; }

  [Property(Name = "Timestamp", Column = "timestamp", NotNull = true)]
  public virtual DateTime Timestamp { get; set; }


[ManyToOne(0, Column = "post_id", NotNull = true, Lazy = Laziness.NoProxy, N
ame = "Post")]
  [Key(1)]
  public virtual Post Post { get; set; }
}
```

And, finally, the **UserDetail** class also needs to be mapped (it is the implementation of the **Details** component of the **User** and **Comment** classes):

```
[Component]
public class UserDetail
{
  [Property(Name = "Url", Column = "url", Length = 50, NotNull = false)]
  public String Url { get; set; }

  [Property(Name = "Fullname",
Column = "fullname", Length = 50, NotNull = true)]
  public String Fullname { get; set; }

  [Property(Name = "Email", Column = "email", Length = 50, NotNull = true)]
  public String Email { get; set; }
}
```

After that, we need to add this kind of mapping to the NHibernate configuration. Here's how:

```
HbmSerializer serializer = new HbmSerializer() { Validate = true };

using (MemoryStream stream = serializer.Serialize(typeof(Blog).Assembly))
{
  cfg.AddInputStream(stream);
}
```

💡 **Tip: Add a reference to the** *System.IO* **and** *NHibernate.Mapping.Attributes* **namespaces.**

For adding parameters to the identifier generator:

```
[Class(Table = "attachment", Lazy = true)]
public class Attachment
{
  [Id(0, Column = "attachment_id", Name = "AttachmentId")]
  [Generator(1, Class = "hilo")]
  [Param(Name = "sequence", Content = "ATTACHMENT_SEQUENCE")]
  public virtual Int32 AttachmentId { get; protected set; }
  //
}
```

And that's it. There are two things of which you must be aware when mapping with attributes:

- For those mappings that need multiple attributes (the collections and the identifiers), you need to set an order on these attributes; that's what the first number on each attribute declaration is for. See, for example, the **Posts** collection of the **Blog** class and its **BlogId** property.
- **Property** attributes need to take the property they are being applied to as their **Name**.

Mapping Inheritances

Consider the following class hierarchy:

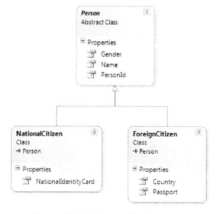

Figure 18: Inheritance Model

We have here an abstract concept, a **Person**, and two concrete representations of it, a **NationalCitizen** and a **ForeignCitizen**. Each **Person** must be one of them. In some countries (like Portugal, for example), there is a National Identity Card, whereas in other countries no such card exists—only a passport and the country of issue.

In object-oriented languages, we have class inheritance, which is something we don't have with relational databases. So a question arises: How can we store this in a relational database?

In his seminal work _Patterns of Enterprise Application Architecture_, Martin Fowler described three patterns for persisting class hierarchies in relational databases:

1. **Single Table Inheritance** or **Table Per Class Hierarchy**: A single table is used to represent the entire hierarchy. It contains columns for all mapped properties of all classes and, of course, many of these will be **NULL** because they will only exist for one particular class. One discriminating column will store a value that will tell NHibernate what class a particular record will map to:

Figure 19: Single Table Inheritance

2. **Class Table Inheritance** or **Table Per Class**: A table will be used for the columns for all mapped-based class properties, and additional tables will exist for all concrete classes. The additional tables will be linked by foreign keys to the base table:

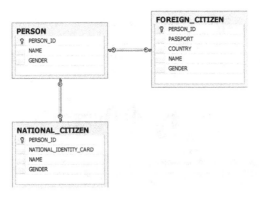

Figure 20: Class Table Inheritance

3. **Concrete Table Inheritance** or **Table Per Concrete Class**: One table for each concrete class, each with columns for all mapped properties specific or inherited by each class:

Figure 21: Concrete Table Inheritance

You can see a more detailed explanation of these patterns in Martin's website at http://martinfowler.com/eaaCatalog/index.html. For now, I'll leave you with some general thoughts:

- **Single Table Inheritance**: When it comes to querying from a base class, this offers the fastest performance because all of the information is contained in a single table. However, if you have a lot of properties in all of the classes, it will be a difficult read and you will have a lot of nullable columns. In all of the concrete classes, all properties must be optional, not mandatory. Since different entities will be stored in the same class and not all share the same columns, they must allow null values.
- **Class Table Inheritance**: This offers a good balance between table tidiness and performance. When querying a base class, a LEFT JOIN will be required to join each table from derived classes to the base class table. A record will exist in the base class table and in exactly one of the derived class tables.
- **Concrete Table Inheritance**: This will require several UNIONs, one for each table of each derived class because NHibernate does not know beforehand at which table to look. Consequently, you cannot use as the identifier generation pattern one that might generate identical values for any two tables (such as identity or sequence, with a sequence being used for each individual table) because NHibernate would be confused if it finds two records with the same id. Also, you will have the same columns—those from the base class—duplicated on all tables.

As far as NHibernate is concerned, there really isn't any difference: classes are naturally polymorphic. See the section on

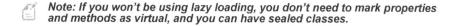

> **Note: If you won't be using lazy loading, you don't need to mark properties and methods as virtual, and you can have sealed classes.**

Inheritance to learn how to perform queries on class hierarchies.

Let's start with Single Table Inheritance, by code. First, the base class, **Person**:

```
public class PersonMapping : ClassMapping<Person>
{
    public PersonMapping()
    {
```

```
    this.Table("person");
    this.Lazy(true);

    this.Discriminator(x =>
    {
      x.Column("class");
      x.NotNullable(true);
    });

    this.Id(x => x.PersonId, x =>
    {
      x.Column("person_id");
      x.Generator(Generators.HighLow);
    });

    this.Property(x => x.Name, x =>
    {
      x.Column("name");
      x.NotNullable(true);
      x.Length(100);
    });

    this.Property(x => x.Gender, x =>
    {
      x.Column("gender");
      x.NotNullable(true);
      x.Type<EnumType<Gender>>();
    });
  }
}
```

The only thing that's new is the **Discriminator** option, which we use to declare the column that will contain the discriminator value for all subclasses.

Next, the mapping for the **NationalCitizen** class:

```
public class NationalCitizenMappping : SubclassMapping<NationalCitizen>
{
  public NationalCitizenMappping()
  {
    this.DiscriminatorValue("national_citizen");
    this.Lazy(true);

    this.Property(x => x.NationalIdentityCard, x =>
    {
      x.Column("national_identity_card");
      x.Length(20);
      x.NotNullable(true);
    });
  }
}
```

And, finally, the **ForeignCitizen**:

```
public class ForeignCitizenMapping : SubclassMapping<ForeignCitizen>
```

```
{
  public ForeignCitizenMapping()
  {
    this.DiscriminatorValue("foreign_citizen");
    this.Lazy(true);

    this.Property(x => x.Country, x =>
    {
      x.Column("country");
      x.Length(20);
      x.NotNullable(true);
    });

    this.Property(x => x.Passport, x =>
    {
      x.Column("passport");
      x.Length(20);
      x.NotNullable(true);
    });
  }
}
```

If you would like to map this by XML, here's one possibility:

```
<hibernate-
mapping namespace="Succinctly.Model" assembly="Succinctly.Model" xmlns="urn:
nhibernate-mapping-2.2">
  <class name="Person" lazy="true" table="`person`" abstract="true">
    <id column="`person_id`" name="PersonId" generator="hilo"/>
    <discriminator column="`class`"/>
    <property name="Name" column="`name`" length="100" not-null="true"/>
    <property name="Gender" column="gender"/>
  </class>
</hibernate-mapping>
```

```
<hibernate-mapping namespace="Succinctly.Model" assembly="Succinctly.Model"
xmlns="urn:nhibernate-mapping-2.2">
  <subclass name="NationalCitizen" lazy="true" extends="Person"
discriminator-value="national_citizen">

<property name="NationalIdentityCard" column="`national_identity_card`" leng
th="20" not-null="false"/>
  </subclass>
</hibernate-mapping>
```

```
<hibernate-mapping namespace="Succinctly.Model" assembly="Succinctly.Model"
xmlns="urn:nhibernate-mapping-2.2">
  <subclass name="ForeignCitizen"
lazy="true" extends="Person" discriminator-value="foreign_citizen">
```

```
    <property name="Country" column="`country`" length="20" not-
null="false"/>
    <property name="Passport" column="`passport`" length="20" not-
null="false"/>
  </subclass>
</hibernate-mapping>
```

And, finally, if your choice is attributes mapping, here's how it goes:

```
[Class(0, Table = "person", Lazy = true, Abstract = true)]
[Discriminator(1, Column = "class")]
public abstract class Person
{
  [Id(0, Name = "PersonId", Column = "person_id")]
  [Generator(1, Class = "hilo")]
  public virtual Int32 PersonId { get; protected set; }

  [Property(Name = "Name", Column = "name", Length = 100, NotNull = true)]
  public virtual String Name { get; set; }


[Property(Name = "Gender", Column = "gender", TypeType = typeof(EnumType<Gen
der>), NotNull = true)]
  public virtual Gender Gender { get; set; }
}
```

```
[Subclass(DiscriminatorValue = "national_citizen", ExtendsType = typeof(Pers
on), Lazy = true)]
public class NationalCitizen : Person
{

[Property(Name = "NationalIdentityCard", Column = "national_identity_card",
Length = 50, NotNull = false)]
  public virtual String NationalIdentityCard { get; set; }
}
```

```
[Subclass(DiscriminatorValue = "foreign_citizen", ExtendsType = typeof(Perso
n), Lazy = true)]
public class ForeignCitizen : Person
{

[Property(Name = "Passport", Column = "passport", Length = 50, NotNull = fal
se)]
  public virtual String Passport { get; set; }


[Property(Name = "Country", Column = "country", Length = 50, NotNull = false
)]
  public virtual String Country { get; set; }
}
```

When it comes to querying, a query on the **Person** class looks like this:

```
IEnumerable<Person> allPeopleFromLinq = session.Query<Person>().ToList();
```

Produces this SQL:

```
SELECT
        person0_.person_id AS person1_2_,
        person0_.name AS name2_,
        person0_.gender AS gender2_,
        person0_.passport AS passport2_,
        person0_.country AS country2_,
        person0_.national_identity_card AS national7_2_,
        person0_.[class] AS class2_2_
FROM
        person person0_
```

If we want to restrict on a specific type:

```
IEnumerable<NationalCitizen> nationalCitizensFromLinq = session.Query<Nation
alCitizen>().ToList();
```

Will produce this SQL:

```
SELECT
    nationalci0_.person_id AS person1_2_,
    nationalci0_.name AS name2_,
    nationalci0_.gender AS gender2_,
    nationalci0_.national_identity_card AS national7_2_
FROM
    person nationalci0_
WHERE
    nationalci0_.[class] = 'national_citizen'
```

Moving on, we have Class Table Inheritance, which is also known in NHibernate jargon as **joined subclass** because we need to join two tables together to get the class' values. Here are its loquacious mappings (the mappings for the **Person** class remain the same, except that we removed the **Discriminator** call):

```
public class PersonMapping : ClassMapping<Person>
{
  public PersonMapping()
  {
    this.Table("person");
    this.Lazy(true);

    this.Id(x => x.PersonId, x =>
    {
      x.Column("person_id");
      x.Generator(Generators.HighLow);
    });
```

```
    this.Property(x => x.Name, x =>
    {
      x.Column("name");
      x.NotNullable(true);
      x.Length(100);
    });

    this.Property(x => x.Gender, x =>
    {
      x.Column("gender");
      x.NotNullable(true);
      x.Type<EnumType<Gender>>();
    });
  }
}
```

```
public class NationalCitizenMappping : JoinedSubclassMapping<NationalCitizen>
{
  public NationalCitizenMappping()
  {

    this.Table("national_citizen");
    this.Lazy(true);

    this.Key(x =>
    {
      x.Column("person_id");
      x.NotNullable(true);
    });

    this.Property(x => x.NationalIdentityCard, x =>
    {
      x.Column("national_identity_card");
      x.Length(20);
      x.NotNullable(true);
    });
  }
}
```

For **ForeignCitizen**:

```
public class ForeignCitizenMapping : JoinedSubclassMapping<ForeignCitizen>
{
  public ForeignCitizenMapping()
  {

    this.Table("foreign_citizen");
    this.Lazy(true);

    this.Key(x =>
    {
```

```
    x.Column("person_id");
    x.NotNullable(true);
  });

  this.Property(x => x.Country, x =>
  {
    x.Column("country");
    x.Length(20);
    x.NotNullable(true);
  });

  this.Property(x => x.Passport, x =>
  {
    x.Column("passport");
    x.Length(20);
    x.NotNullable(true);
  });
  }
}
```

Here, what's different in the mapping of the subclasses is the introduction of a **Key**, which we use to tell NHibernate the column to use for joining with the **PERSON** table.

The XML equivalent would be:

```
<hibernate-
mapping namespace="Succinctly.Model" assembly="Succinctly.Model" xmlns="urn:
nhibernate-mapping-2.2">
  <class name="Person" lazy="true" table="`PERSON`" abstract="true">
    <id column="`PERSON_ID`" name="PersonId" generator="hilo"/>
    <property name="Name" column="`name`" length="100" not-null="true"/>
    <property name="Gender" column="gender"/>
  </class>
</hibernate-mapping>
```

```
<hibernate-
mapping namespace="Succinctly.Model" assembly="Succinctly.Model" xmlns="urn:
nhibernate-mapping-2.2">
  <joined-
subclass name="NationalCitizen" lazy="true" extends="Person" table="`NATIONA
L_CITIZEN`">
    <key column="`PERSON_ID`"/>

<property name="NationalIdentityCard" column="`national_identity_card`" leng
th="20" not-null="false"/>
  </joined-subclass>
</hibernate-mapping>
```

```
<hibernate-
mapping namespace="Succinctly.Model" assembly="Succinctly.Model" xmlns="urn:
nhibernate-mapping-2.2">
  <joined-
subclass name="ForeignCitizen" lazy="true" extends="Person" table="`FOREIGN_
CITIZEN`">
    <key column="`PERSON_ID`"/>
    <property name="Country" column="`country`" length="20" not-
null="false"/>
    <property name="Passport" column="`passport`" length="20" not-
null="false"/>
  </joined-subclass>
</hibernate-mapping>
```

Finally, the attributes version:

```
[Class(0, Table = "person", Lazy = true, Abstract = true)]
public abstract class Person
{
  //…
}
```

```
[JoinedSubclass(0, Table = "national_citizen", ExtendsType = typeof(Person),
 Lazy = true)]
[Key(1, Column = "person_id")]
public class NationalCitizen : Person
{
  //…
}
```

```
[JoinedSubclass(0, Table = "foreign_citizen", ExtendsType = typeof(Person),
Lazy = true)]
[Key(1, Column = "person_id")]
public class ForeignCitizen : Person
{
  //…
}
```

A query for the base class produces the following SQL, joining all tables together:

```
SELECT
    person0_.person_id AS person1_6_,
    person0_.name AS name6_,
    person0_.gender AS gender6_,
    person0_1_.passport AS passport11_,
    person0_1_.country AS country11_,
    person0_2_.national_identity_card AS national2_12_,
    CASE
        WHEN person0_1_.person_id IS NOT NULL THEN 1
```

```
        WHEN person0_2_.person_id IS NOT NULL THEN 2
        WHEN person0_.person_id IS NOT NULL THEN 0
    END AS clazz_
FROM
    person person0_
LEFT OUTER JOIN
    foreign_citizen person0_1_
        ON person0_.person_id = person0_1_.person_id
LEFT OUTER JOIN
    national_citizen person0_2_
        ON person0_.person_id = person0_2_.person_id
```

And one for a specific class:

```
SELECT
    nationalci0_.person_id AS person1_2_,
    nationalci0_1_.name AS name2_,
    nationalci0_1_.gender AS gender2_,
    nationalci0_.national_identity_card AS national2_8_
FROM
    national_citizen nationalci0_
INNER JOIN
    person nationalci0_1_
        ON nationalci0_.person_id = nationalci0_1_.person_id
```

Finally, the last mapping strategy, Concrete Table Inheritance or **union-subclass**. The mappings, using the loquacious API:

```
public class NationalCitizenMappping : UnionSubclassMapping<NationalCitizen>
{
  public NationalCitizenMappping()
  {
    this.Table("national_citizen");
    this.Lazy(true);
    //...
  }
}
```

```
public class ForeignCitizenMappping : UnionSubclassMapping<ForeignCitizen>
{
  public ForeignCitizenMappping()
  {
    this.Table("foreign_citizen");
    this.Lazy(true);
    //...
  }
}
```

 Tip: The mapping for Person *is exactly the same as for the Class Table Inheritance.*

As you can see, the only difference is that the **Key** entry is now gone. That's it.

Also in XML:

```xml
<hibernate-mapping namespace="Succinctly.Model" assembly="Succinctly.Model"
xmlns="urn:nhibernate-mapping-2.2">
  <union-
subclass name="NationalCitizen" lazy="true" extends="Person" table="`NATIONA
L_CITIZEN`">
    <!-- … -->
  </union-subclass>
</hibernate-mapping>
```

```xml
<hibernate-mapping namespace="Succinctly.Model" assembly="Succinctly.Model"
xmlns="urn:nhibernate-mapping-2.2">
  <union-
subclass name="ForeignCitizen" lazy="true" extends="Person" table="`FOREIGN_
CITIZEN`">
    <!-- … -->
  </union-subclass>
</hibernate-mapping>
```

And in attributes:

```csharp
[UnionSubclass(0, Table = "national_citizen", ExtendsType = typeof(Person),
Lazy = true)]
public class NationalCitizen : Person
{
  //…
}
```

```csharp
[UnionSubclass(0, Table = "foreign_citizen", ExtendsType = typeof(Person), L
azy = true)]
public class ForeignCitizen : Person
{
  //…
}
```

At the end of this section, let's see what the SQL for the base **Person** class looks like when using this strategy:

```sql
SELECT
    person0_.person_id AS person1_6_,
    person0_.name AS name6_,
    person0_.gender AS gender6_,
    person0_.passport AS passport11_,
    person0_.country AS country11_,
    person0_.national_identity_card AS national1_12_,
```

```
      person0_.clazz_ AS clazz_
FROM
    ( SELECT
        person_id,
        name,
        gender,
        passport,
        country,
        null AS national_identity_card,
        1 AS clazz_
    FROM
        foreign_citizen
    UNION
    ALL SELECT
        person_id,
        name,
        gender,
        null AS passport,
        null AS country,
        national_identity_card,
        2 AS clazz_
    FROM
        national_citizen
) person0_
```

And a query for a particular class, in this case, **NationalCitizen** will produce the following SQL:

```
SELECT
    nationalci0_.person_id AS person1_6_,
    nationalci0_.name AS name6_,
    nationalci0_.gender AS gender6_,
    nationalci0_.national_identity_card AS national1_12_
FROM
    national_citizen nationalci0_
```

Which One Shall I Choose?

We have seen a lot of things in this chapter. For mapping APIs, I risk offering my opinion: choose mapping by code. It is more readable and easy to maintain than **HBM.XML**, and it is strongly typed, meaning that, if you change some property, you will automatically refactor the mapping and won't need to bother to explicitly compile your project because, since it's code, Visual Studio will do it whenever necessary. Attributes require a reference to a NHibernate-specific assembly and are more difficult to change than mapping by code.

In the end, with whatever mapping you choose, here is the resulting database model:

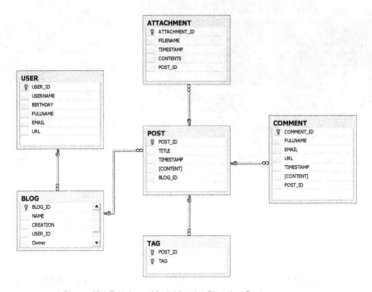

Figure 22: Database Model for the Blogging System

For mapping inheritances, it is a decision worth thinking over, as there is no direct answer. But I am in favor of **Class Table Inheritance** because there is no duplication of columns for each concrete class and because each table only has a few columns.

Chapter 5 Querying the Database

Granted, probably the most typical operation you do involving a database is to query it. NHibernate offers a rich set of APIs to do this, covering different use cases.

To start querying your model, you need a session. A session is obtained from a session factory which, in turn, is built from the configuration object you learned to create in the chapter on Chapter 2 Configuration. You will use something like:

```
//the one and only session factory
using (ISessionFactory sessionFactory = cfg.BuildSessionFactory())
{
  using (ISession session = sessionFactory.OpenSession())
  {
    //one session
  }

  using (ISession session = sessionFactory.OpenSession())
  {
    //another session
  }
}
```

Tip: You will need to reference the NHibernate namespace in order to compile this example.

Do note that both the session factory and the sessions are wrapped in **using** blocks. This is to ensure that they both are disposed of when no longer needed—at the end of each block.

A session factory may spawn multiple-session objects. It is a heavy beast and, typically, you only have one of these in your program. You will only need more than one if you wish to target multiple databases at the same time. In that case, there will be multiple Configuration and ISessionFactory instances. It is safe to access a session factory from multiple threads. What's a session factory used for? Well, it builds up all the metadata from the mappings in the configuration object and tries to match them against actual .NET classes and database tables. It is the session factory that triggers the data model creation/validation that was discussed at the start of the Chapter 3 Domain Model

Scenario

Let's consider a simple model, a blogging system:

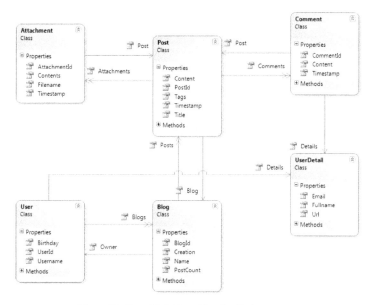

Figure 23: Class Model for a Blogging System

It can be described as this: A **Blog** is owned by a **User** and has a collection of **Posts**. Each **Post** may have **Comments** and **Attachments**, each referring to a single **Post**. A **User** may have several **Blogs**. Both **User** and **Comment** have **UserDetails**.

Occasionally, I will also refer another model, a classical ordering system, which will look like this:

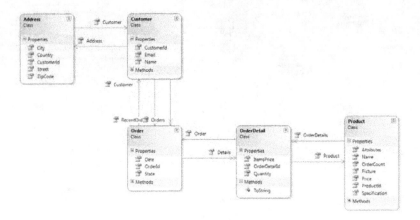

Figure 24: Class Model for the Orders System

These are the concepts that we will want to represent and manipulate in our code. However, I will only include code for the blogging model. You will be able to find the classes and mappings for the ordering model on the book's Bitbucket repository.

Entities

We have several ways to represent these concepts. I chose one. Here are the classes that we will be using throughout the book:

The **User** class:

```
public class User
{
  public User()
  {
    this.Blogs = new Iesi.Collections.Generic.HashedSet<Blog>();
    this.Details = new UserDetail();
  }

  public virtual Int32 UserId { get; protected set;}

  public virtual String Username { get; set; }

  public virtual UserDetail Details { get; set; }

  public virtual DateTime? Birthday { get; set; }

  public virtual Iesi.Collections.Generic.ISet<Blog> Blogs { get;
protected set; }
}
```

The **Blog** class:

```
public class Blog
{
    public Blog()
    {
        this.Posts = new List<Post>();
    }

    public virtual Int32 BlogId { get; protected set; }

    public virtual System.Drawing.Image Picture { get; set; }

    public virtual Int64 PostCount { get; protected set; }

    public virtual User Owner { get; set; }

    public virtual String Name { get; set; }

    public virtual DateTime Creation { get; set; }

    public virtual IList<Post> Posts { get; protected set; }
}
```

Tip: Because the Blog class has a property of type System.Drawing.Image, *you need to add a reference to the* System.Drawing *assembly.*

The **Post** class:

```
public class Post
{
    public Post()
    {
        this.Tags = new Iesi.Collections.Generic.HashedSet<String>();
        this.Attachments = new Iesi.Collections.Generic.HashedSet<Attachment>();
        this.Comments = new List<Comment>();
    }

    public virtual Int32 PostId { get; protected set; }

    public virtual Blog Blog { get; set; }

    public virtual DateTime Timestamp { get; set; }

    public virtual String Title { get; set; }

    public virtual String Content { get; set; }

    public virtual Iesi.Collections.Generic.ISet<String> Tags { get;
protected set; }

    public virtual Iesi.Collections.Generic.ISet<Attachment> Attachments {
get; protected set; }
```

```
    public virtual IList<Comment> Comments { get; protected set; }
}
```

The **Comment** class:

```
public class Comment
{
    public Comment()
    {
        this.Details = new UserDetail();
    }

    public virtual Int32 CommentId { get; protected set; }

    public virtual UserDetail Details { get; set; }

    public virtual DateTime Timestamp { get; set; }

    public virtual String Content { get; set; }

    public virtual Post Post { get; set; }
}
```

The **Attachment** class:

```
public class Attachment
{
    public virtual Int32 AttachmentId { get; protected set; }

    public virtual String Filename { get; set; }

    public virtual Byte[] Contents { get; set; }

    public virtual DateTime Timestamp { get; set; }

    public virtual Post Post { get; set; }
}
```

And, finally, the **UserDetail** class (it is the implementation of the **Details** component of the **User** and **Comment** classes):

```
public class UserDetail
{
    public String Url { get; set; }

    public String Fullname { get; set; }

    public String Email { get; set; }
}
```

Some notes:

- As you can see, there is no base class or special interface that we need to implement. This does not mean that NHibernate can't use them; it is actually quite the opposite.
- All classes are non-sealed. This is not strictly a requirement but a recommended practice.
- Some properties are virtual, basically all except those from the **UserDetail** component class. Also, a recommended practice; we will see why when we talk about lazy loading in the next chapter.
- Properties that will represent the primary key have a protected setter. This is because NHibernate will be providing this key for us so there is no need. In fact, it is dangerous to change it.
- Collections also have protected setters because the operations that we will be performing with them won't require changing the actual collection reference, but rather, merely adding, removing, and eventually clearing it.
- All collections are instantiated in the constructor of their declaring classes so that they are never **null**.

Before We Start

Because NHibernate is an ORM, it will transform tables into classes, columns into properties, and records into object instances and values. Exactly how this transformation occurs depends on the mapping. A mapping is something that you add to the configuration instance. You can add multiple mappings—typically one for each .NET class that you want to be able to persist to the database. At the very minimum, a mapping must associate a table name to a class name, the column that contains the primary key to a related class property, and probably some additional columns into the properties they will be turned to.

As far as NHibernate is concerned, an entity is just a Plain Old CLR Object (POCO). You have to make a fundamental choice when it comes to creating these entities:

- You start from code, following a Domain Driven Design (DDD) approach. You define your classes without much concern about how they will be stored in the database. Instead, you focus on getting them right. This may include creating inheritance relationships and complex properties.
- You start from the database and you have to craft your entities so that they match the data model. This may be because it's the way your company works, you have a legacy database, or it is just a matter of personal preference.

We won't go into what is the best approach; that is up to you. Either way is fully supported by NHibernate. If you start from code, NHibernate will happily generate the database for you or validate it. In both cases—database first or code first—NHibernate will also give you the option to check the database against your entities and either update the database to match the entities or warn you if there are discrepancies. There's a **SchemaAction** setting for this on the **Configuration** class, using loquacious configuration:

```
Configuration cfg = new Configuration()
.DataBaseIntegration(db =>
{
    //…
    db.SchemaAction = SchemaAutoAction.Validate;
```

```
})
```

As well as in XML configuration, as a property:

```
<property name="hbm2ddl.auto">validate</property>
```

The possible values you can pass to **SchemaAction/hbm2ddl.auto** are:

- **Create/create**: Will always drop existing tables and recreate them from the current mappings.
- **Recreate/create-drop**: Identical to **Create,** with the difference being that it will drop everything again when NHibernate finishes using the database (the session factory is disposed of).
- **Update/update**: NHibernate will compare the existing tables to the current mappings and will update the database, if necessary, including creating missing tables or columns.
- **Validate/validate**: An exception will be thrown if the comparison between the actual tables and the current mapping detects mismatches.

 Tip: Create and Recreate are dangerous, and you should only use them for scenarios such as unit tests or demonstrations where you need to quickly set up a database or where you have no important information because every mapped table will be dropped—not mapped tables will be left alone, though. Update will also create any missing tables and columns so it is safe to use in real-life scenarios, but it may take some time to check all tables if you have a lot of mapped classes. If no value is set by calling SchemaAction or by setting the hbm2ddl.auto attribute on the XML configuration, no validation will be performed and no schema update/creation will occur.

Chapter 4 Mappings chapter. And it is its disposal that will trigger its dropping, if so configured. It is read-only.

 Note: Do not make changes to the Configuration **instance after creating a session factory.**

Sessions, on the other hand, are lightweight and do not actually represent a connection to a database; one is created when necessary, automatically. A session is where the action actually occurs. It's the session that is responsible for querying. They are lightweight, so you can create new instances whenever you need them, typically inside a method. Do not keep references to a session in places where it might not be released. Also, do not access sessions from different threads; unexpected behavior may occur.

 Tip: Whenever an exception is thrown by any session operation, the session instance becomes unusable and must be disposed of.

That being said, there are several APIs that will take a query and return a collection of in-memory objects that map to the objects on your database. Let's look at them one by one.

Before we start, this is the domain model that we will be using:

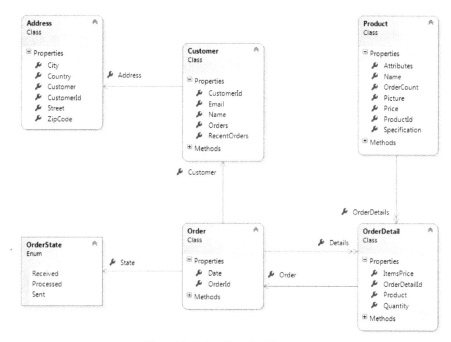

Figure 25: Orders Class Model

By ID

If you know the identifier of the record you are trying to obtain, you can get it directly by this id:

```
//get strongly typed instance by id
var someProduct = session.Get<Product>(1);

//get object instance by id and type
var someObject = session.Get(typeof(Product), 1);
```

Get will return **null** if the record is not found. If it is, it will be loaded from the database and the appropriate class materialized.

LINQ

Since .NET 3.5 came along, LINQ has become the de facto standard for querying in the .NET world and it is understandable why. It is a unified way of performing strongly typed, object-oriented queries that are independent of the data source. NHibernate, of course, supports LINQ querying. To issue a LINQ query, you must make use of the **Query** extension method applied to a session:

```
//simplest LINQ query containing a filter
var products = session.Query<Product>().Where(x => x.Price > 1000).ToList();
```

 Tip: Import the NHibernate, NHibernate.Linq, *and* System.Linq *namespaces.*

Keep in mind that a LINQ query is only executed (sent to the database) when a terminal method is called such as **ToList**, **ToArray**, **Single**, **SingleOrDefault**, **First**, **FirstOrDefault**, **Any** or **Count**. If you don't include such a method call, all you have is a query waiting to be executed, and you can add conditions and ordering to it:

```
//a query over all Products
var allProductsQuery = session.Query<Product>();

if (someCondition == true)
{
  //a filter
  allProductsQuery = allProductsQuery.Where(x => x.Price > 1000);
}
else
{
  //a filter
  allProductsQuery = allProductsQuery.Where(x => x.Price <= 1000);
}

if (sortByName == true)
{
  //ordering
  allProductsQuery = allProductsQuery.OrderBy(x => x.Name);
}
else
{
  //ordering
  allProductsQuery = allProductsQuery.OrderByDescending(x => x.Price);
}

//run the query
var allProducts = allProductsQuery.ToList();
```

LINQ supports most operations available on SQL, for example:

```
//checking if a record exists
```

```
var productsWithoutOrders = session.Query<Product>().Where(x => x.OrderDetai
ls.Any() == false).ToList();

//filter on collection
var ordersOfIphones = session.Query<OrderDetail>().Where(x => x.Product.Name
 == "iPhone")
.Select(x => x.Order).ToList();

//two optional conditions
var processedOrReceivedOrders = session.Query<Order>()
.Where(x => x.State == OrderState.Processed || x.State == OrderState.Receive
d).ToList();

//grouping and counting
var countByProduct = (from od in session.Query<OrderDetail>()
                group od by od.Product.Name into p
                select new { Product = p.Key, Count = p.Count() })
                .ToList();

//customers with two orders
var customersWithTwoOrders = session.Query<Customer>().Where(x => x.Orders.C
ount() == 2)
.ToList();

//nesting queries
var customersWithOrders = session.Query<Customer>().Where(x => x.Orders.Any(
));

var ordersFromCustomers = session.Query<Order>().Where(x => customersWithOrd
ers
.Contains(x.Customer))
.ToList();

//paging
var productsFrom20to30 = session.Query<Product>().Skip(19).Take(10).ToList()
;

//multiple conditions
var productsWithPriceBetween10And20 = session.Query<Product>()
.Where(x => x.Price >= 10 && x.Price < 20)
.ToList();

//first record that matches a condition
var customerWithMoreOrders = session.Query<Customer>().OrderBy(x => x.Orders
.Count())
.FirstOrDefault();

//projection
var productsAndOrderCount = session.Query<Product>()
.Select(x => new { x.Name, Count = x.OrderDetails.Count() }).ToList();

//theta join with projection
var productsAndCustomers = (from p in session.Query<Product>()
        join od in session.Query<OrderDetail>() on p equals od.Product
        select new { ProductName = p.Name, CustomerName = od.Order.Customer.
Name })
.ToList().Distinct();
```

```
//property navigation and sorting
var firstCustomer = session.Query<OrderDetail>().OrderBy(x => x.Order.Date)
.Select(x => x.Order.Customer.Name).FirstOrDefault();

//set of values
var orders = session.Query<Order>()
.Where(x => new OrderState[] { OrderState.Processed, OrderState.Sent }.Conta
ins(x.State))
.ToList();

//parameters
var recentOrders = session.Query<Order>()
.Where(x => x.Date <= DateTime.Today && x.Date > DateTime.Today.AddDays(-
7)).ToList();
```

One notable exception that NHibernate LINQ cannot handle is OUTER JOINs (LEFT, RIGHT, FULL). In the current version of NHibernate, OUTER JOINs between unrelated entities are not supported.

 Note: Do not be alarmed by the presence of constants; all constants will be translated to parameters so as to reuse the execution plan for the query. This also prevents SQL injection.

Most users of NHibernate will use LINQ as its primary query API, but there are alternatives as we will see next.

HQL

Hibernate Query Language (HQL) is a database-independent, object-oriented, SQL-like language that can be used for general-purpose querying over entities. Its syntax is very similar to SQL as you can see for yourself:

 Tip: To try these examples, import the NHibernate namespace.

```
//checking if a record exists
var productsWithoutOrders = session.CreateQuery(
"from Product x where not exists elements(x.OrderDetails)").List<Product>();

//filter on collection
var ordersOfIphones = session.CreateQuery(
"select o from Order o join o.Details od where od.Product.Name = :name").Set
Parameter("name", "iPhone")
.List<Order>();

//two optional conditions
var processedOrReceivedOrders = session.CreateQuery(
"from Order o where o.State = :processed or o.State = :received")
```

```
.SetParameter("processed", OrderState.Processed).SetParameter("received", Or
derState.Received)
.List<Order>();

//grouping and counting
var countByProduct = session.CreateQuery(
"select od.Product.Name, count(od) from OrderDetail od group by od.Product.N
ame").List<Object[]>();

//customers with two orders
var customersWithTwoOrders = session.CreateQuery("from Customer c where c.Or
ders.size = 2")
.List<Customer>();

//nesting queries
var ordersFromCustomers = session.CreateQuery(
"from Order o where o.Customer in (select c from Customer c where exists ele
ments(c.Orders))")
.List<Order>();

//paging
var productsFrom20to30 = session.CreateQuery("from Product skip 19 take 10")
.List<Product>();
//this is identical
var productsFrom20to30 = session.CreateQuery("from Product").SetMaxResults(1
0)
.SetFirstResult(20)
.List<Product>();

//theta joins with projection
var productCustomer = session.CreateQuery(
"select distinct p.Name, od.Order.Customer.Name from Product p, OrderDetail
od where od.Product = p")
.List<Object[]>();

//property navigation and sorting
var firstCustomerWith = session.CreateQuery(
"select x.Order.Customer.Name from OrderDetail x order by x.Order.Date take
1")
.UniqueResult<String>();

//set of values
var orders = session.CreateQuery("from Order o where o.State in (:states)")
.SetParameterList("states", new OrderState[] { OrderState.Processed,OrderSta
te.Sent }).List<Order>();

//parameters
var recentOrders = session
.CreateQuery("from Order o where o.Date between :today and :a_week_ago")
.SetParameter("today", DateTime.Today).SetParameter("a_week_ago", DateTime.T
oday.AddDays(-7))
.List<Order>();
```

But beware! While HQL itself is case-insensitive ("select" is equal to "SELECT" is equal to
"Select") the class' names and properties are not.

Similar to LINQ, you can take the **IQuery** object and add paging (**SetFirstResult**, **SetMaxResults**) or parameters (**SetParameter**, **SetParameterList**, **SetEntity**) before actually executing the query, which will only happen when you call **List**, **List<T>**, **UniqueResult** or **UniqueResult<T>**. You will probably want to use the generic version of these methods when your query returns entities. In this case, because the HQL query is not strongly typed, you need to set the generic parameter type yourself.

A parameter in HQL is always specified with the **':'** character as a prefix to its name, regardless of the character that the database uses (**'@'** in Oracle, **':'** in SQL Server, etc). Its position does not matter, only its name. If the parameter is a single value, you should use **SetParameter** to set its value; if it is a collection (array, **ArrayList** or **List<T>**), use **SetParameterList** instead. If you are passing an entity, use **SetEntity**.

One advantage that HQL offers is that it has access to standard SQL functions, although probably with a nonstandard name. Here are some of them, available for all database engines:

Category	Function	Description
Aggregations	count(...)	Count of items
	count(distinct ...)	Count of distinct items
	max(...)	Maximum value
	min(...)	Minimum value
	sum(...)	Sum of all values
	avg(...)	Average of all values
Date and Time	day(...)	Day part of a date
	month(...)	Month part of a date
	year(...)	Year part of a date
	hour(...)	Hours part of a date/time
	minute(...)	Minutes part of a date/time
	second(...)	Seconds part of a date/time
	extract(... from ...)	Extracts a part from a date/time
	current_timestamp	Current database date and time

Category	Function	Description
General Purpose	cast(…)	Casts an expression into another .NET type
	coalesce(…)	Returns the first non-null value
	nullif(…)	If two values are equal, returns null
	id	Entity identifier
	size	Collection size
	class	Returns the actual class of an abstract entity
Mathematics	sqrt(…)	Square root
	log(…)	Natural logarithm
	tan(…)	Tangent
	sin(…)	Sine
	cos(…)	Cosine
	mod(…)	Modulus, the remaining of an integer division
	rand()	Random value
	abs(…)	Absolute value
String	concat(…)	Concatenates several strings together
	substring(…)	Returns a substring
	locate(…)	Returns the index of a substring
	replace(…)	Replaces the first occurrence of a string
	trim(…)	Removes leading or trailing blank characters
	upper(…)	Uppercase
	lower(…)	Lowercase
	length(…)	Length in characters
	bit_length(…)	Length in bits (length() * 8)
	str(…)	Converts an expression to a string

Some things are different from SQL:

- Outer joins (LEFT, RIGHT, FULL) between two arbitrary, non-related entities are not supported; HQL can only perform joins between entities having properties that link them.
- No "*" selection; the default is to select all of the mapped entities' properties.
- No need to explicitly join two entities whose relation is mapped, just navigate from one to the other through its navigation property.
- All selects must come from some entity, although they might not reference it (for example, "SELECT GETDATE()" is not supported, but "select current_timestamp from Product" is.
- The "select" part is optional; if not present, it means "select all of the mapped entity's properties".
- HQL is polymorphic; it understands base classes, which means that the query "from System.Object" will return all records from the database, so beware!
- You don't have to explicitly escape entities and properties with reserved names (such as **Order**); NHibernate will do it for you.
- If you explicitly join several associations or collections causing a Cartesian product, you may receive a response that is not what you expect: NHibernate will be confused and you will have to tell it to distinguish the distinct root entity that you want, by using a result transformer:

```
//multiple joins
var orderDetailsWithProductsAndOrders = session
.CreateQuery("from OrderDetail od join od.Order join od.Product join
od.Order.Customer")
.SetResultTransformer(Transformers.DistinctRootEntity).List<OrderDetail>();
```

 Tip: Import namespace NHibernate.Transform.

These other things also apply to HQL:

- You should limit the number of records to return, and even use projections, for performance's sake.
- You should use parameters instead of constants, to allow for execution plan reusing.
- HQL is case-insensitive.
- You must use the syntax "is null" instead of "= null".

Criteria

Another querying API is Criteria. It is interesting because it offers a more conceptual, explicit, step-by-step approach, which is good for multi-step dynamic generation of queries. For example:

Tip: *Import the namespaces* NHibernate *and* NHibernate.Criterion.

```
//mixing SQL
var productsByNameLike = session.CreateCriteria(typeof(Product))
.Add(Expression.Sql("Name LIKE ?", "%Phone",
NHibernateUtil.String)).List<Product>();

//checking if a record exists
var productsWithoutOrders = session.CreateCriteria("Product", "p")
.Add(Restrictions.IsEmpty("p.OrderDetails")).List<Product>();

//filter on collection
var ordersOfIphones = session.CreateCriteria(typeof(Order))
.CreateCriteria("Details").CreateCriteria("Product")
.Add(Restrictions.Eq(Projections.Property("Name"), "iPhone")).List<Order>();

//two optional conditions
var processedOrReceivedOrders = session.CreateCriteria(typeof(Order))
.Add(Restrictions.Or(Restrictions.Eq(Projections.Property("State"), OrderSta
te.Processed),
Restrictions.Eq(Projections.Property("State"), OrderState.Received))).List<O
rder>();

//grouping and counting
var projection = Projections.ProjectionList()
.Add(Projections.GroupProperty("p.Name")).Add(Projections.Count("Product"));

var countByProduct = session.CreateCriteria(typeof(OrderDetail), "od")
.CreateAlias("od.Product", "p").SetProjection(projection).List();

//customers with two orders
var innerQuery = DetachedCriteria.For(typeof(Customer))
.CreateAlias("Orders", "o").SetProjection(Projections.ProjectionList()
.Add(Projections.RowCount()));

var customersWithTwoOrders = session.CreateCriteria(typeof(Customer), "c")
.Add(Subqueries.Eq(2, innerQuery)).List<Customer>();

//nesting queries
var innerQuery = DetachedCriteria.For(typeof(Customer), "ic")
.Add(Restrictions.IsNotEmpty("Orders")).SetProjection(Projections.Projection
List()
.Add(Projections.Constant(1)));

var ordersFromCustomers = session.CreateCriteria(typeof(Order), "o")
.Add(Subqueries.Exists(innerQuery))
.List<Order>();

//paging
var productsFrom20to30 = session.CreateCriteria(typeof(Product)).SetMaxResul
ts(10)
.SetFirstResult(20)
.List<Product>();
```

```
//theta joins are not supported by Criteria

//property navigation and sorting
var firstCustomer = session.CreateCriteria(typeof(OrderDetail), "od")
.CreateAlias("Order", "o")
.CreateAlias("o.Customer", "c").SetProjection(Projections.Property("c.Name")
)
.AddOrder(Order.Asc("o.Date")).SetMaxResults(1).UniqueResult<String>();

//set of values
var orders = session.CreateCriteria(typeof(Order))
.Add(Restrictions.In(Projections.Property("State"), new Object[] { OrderStat
e.Processed,
OrderState.Sent })).List<Order>();

//parameters
var recentOrders = session.CreateCriteria(typeof(Order), "o")
.Add(Restrictions.Between(Projections.Property("Date"), DateTime.Today.AddDa
ys(7),
DateTime.Today))
.List<Order>();
```

As you can see, querying with Criteria can be less intuitive than using HQL and LINQ. It requires careful consideration of what to do and may require doing things in several steps, perhaps resorting to additional **DetachedCriteria** objects. The resulting code is normally longer and harder to follow.

Paging works the exact same way by means of **SetMaxResults** and **SetFirstResult**.

You can work exclusively with **DetachedCriterias**, which you can pass around different layers of your application, or even serialize, because they are not tied to any session. In fact, they are a good implementation of the Query Object pattern. One example would be:

```
//checking if a record exists
var productsWithoutOrdersWithDetached = DetachedCriteria.For(typeof(Product)
, "p")
.Add(Restrictions.IsEmpty("p.OrderDetails"));
var productsWithoutOrders = productsWithoutOrdersWithDetached.GetExecutableC
riteria(session)
.List<Product>();
```

If you issue several joins, causing a Cartesian product, you have the same problem that you have with HQL in that you have to tell NHibernate to distinguish the root entity. Here's how to do it with Criteria:

```
//multiple joins
var orderDetailsWithProductsAndOrders = session.CreateCriteria(typeof(OrderD
etail), "od")
.CreateAlias("od.Order", "o").CreateAlias("od.Product", "p").CreateAlias("o.
Customer", "c")
.SetResultTransformer(Transformers.DistinctRootEntity).List<OrderDetail>();
```

Criteria also offers an interesting query possibility, one that does not exist in any of the previous APIs: querying by example. Let's see how this works:

```
//by example
var productsWithSamePrice = session.CreateCriteria(typeof(Product))
.Add(Example.Create(new Product() { Price = 1000 })).List<Product>();
```

Querying by example will take an object and check all of its properties that have non-default values (the id property and collections are not considered) to see what to query for. It will then try to find all objects that match the given values.

Query Over

Next in line is Query Over. It is something of a mix between LINQ and Criteria, meaning it has the same advantages (strong typing, easy to build dynamic queries) and disadvantages (verbosity, complex syntax, need to explicitly perform JOINs). Here are the same queries, now written with Query Over:

 Tip: Import the NHibernate.Criterion **namespace.**

```
//checking if a record exists
var productsWithoutOrders = session.QueryOver<Product>()
.WithSubquery.WhereExists(QueryOver.Of<OrderDetail>().Select(x => x.Product)
).List();

//filter on collection
OrderDetail orderDetailAlias = null;
Product productAlias = null;

var ordersOfIphones = session.QueryOver<Order>().JoinQueryOver(x => x.Detail
s,
() => orderDetailAlias)
.JoinQueryOver(x => x.Product, () => productAlias).Where(x => x.Name == "iPh
one").List();

//two optional conditions
var processedOrReceivedOrders = session.QueryOver<Order>()
.Where(x => x.State == OrderState.Processed || x.State == OrderState.Receive
d).List();

//grouping and counting
Product productAlias = null;

var projection = session.QueryOver<OrderDetail>().JoinAlias(x => x.Product,
() => productAlias)
.SelectList(list => list.SelectGroup(x => productAlias.Name).SelectCount(x =
> x.OrderDetailId))
.List<Object[]>();

//customers with two orders
```

```
var innerQuery = QueryOver.Of<Customer>().JoinQueryOver(x => x.Orders).ToRow
CountQuery();

var customersWithTwoOrders = session.QueryOver<Customer>().WithSubquery.Wher
eValue(2)
.Eq(innerQuery)
.List();

//nesting queries
var innerQuery = QueryOver.Of<Customer>().WhereRestrictionOn(x => x.Orders).
Not.IsEmpty
.Select(x => 1);

var ordersFromCustomers = session.QueryOver<Order>().WithSubquery.WhereExist
s(innerQuery)
.List();

//paging
var productsFrom20to30 = session.QueryOver<Product>().Skip(20).Take(10).List
();

//theta joins are not supported by Criteria

//property navigation and sorting
Order orderAlias = null;
Customer customerAlias = null;

var firstCustomer = session.QueryOver<OrderDetail>().JoinAlias(x => x.Order,
 () => orderAlias)
.JoinAlias(x => x.Order.Customer, () => customerAlias).OrderBy(x => orderAli
as.Date).Desc
.Select(x => customerAlias.Name).Take(1).SingleOrDefault<String>();

//set of values
var orders = session.QueryOver<Order>().WhereRestrictionOn(x => x.State)
.IsIn(new Object[] { OrderState.Processed, OrderState.Sent }).List();

//parameters
var recentOrders = session.QueryOver<Order>()
.Where(Restrictions.Between(Projections.Property<Order>(x => x.Date),
DateTime.Today.AddDays(-7), DateTime.Today)).List();
```

As you can see, Query Over is similar to Criteria but with strongly typed, LINQ-style expressions. Some of these expressions are also entirely compatible with LINQ. Since most are strongly typed, so are aliases and hence the need for helper variables for representing these aliases.

Criteria does not support all of the query possibilities that HQL does, namely, theta joins, which are arbitrary joins between two unrelated tables.

If you ever need to mix Criteria with Query Over, it is possible by means of the **RootCriteria** property:

```
//filter on association by using Criteria
var ordersOfSomeCustomer = session.QueryOver<Order>()
```

```
.JoinQueryOver(x => x.Details, () => orderDetailAlias).RootCriteria
.CreateAlias("Customer", "c")
.Add(Restrictions.Eq(Projections.Property("c.Name"), "Some Name")).List();
```

Querying by example is also supported:

```
//by example
var productsWithSamePrice = session.QueryOver<Product>()
.Where(Example.Create(new Product() { Price = 1000 })).List();
```

Finally, the problem with Cartesian products is also pertinent. Here is the workaround:

```
//multiple joins
OrderDetail orderDetailAlias = null;
Order orderAlias = null;
Product productAlias = null;
Customer customerAlias = null;

var orderDetailsWithProductsAndOrders = session.QueryOver<OrderDetail>(() =>
  orderDetailAlias)
.JoinAlias(x => x.Order, () => orderAlias).JoinAlias(x => x.Product, () => p
roductAlias)
.JoinAlias(x => x.Order.Customer, () => customerAlias)
.TransformUsing(Transformers.DistinctRootEntity)
.List();
```

SQL

The previous querying APIs can be powerful but they are obviously no match for SQL. SQL is the native language of the relational database and is the one that unleashes its full power. Of course, NHibernate also supports SQL querying!

The previous examples should be fairly simple to implement with SQL. Let's look at some examples:

```
var productsNameAndPrice = session.CreateSQLQuery("SELECT p.Name, p.Price FR
OM Product p").List();
var lastWeekOrderDates = session.CreateSQLQuery(
"SELECT o.Date FROM Order o WHERE o.Date > DATEADD(DAY, -
7, GETDATE())").List();
```

You might have noticed that, on the second query, we are using the **DATEADD** and **GETDATE** functions, which are specific to SQL Server. NHibernate lets you do this; it just passes whatever query you give it to the database.

In general, when you use SQL, you might be bringing columns that do not correspond to the ones that your entities are using. So there is no immediate conversion: you are bringing columns, not entities. This is possible, however, by using a special syntax:

```
//mapping columns to entities
```

```
var products = session.CreateSQLQuery("SELECT {p.*} FROM Product p").AddEnti
ty("p", typeof(Product))
.List<Product>();
```

You need to wrap the table or alias containing the entity columns that you wish to materialize inside {} and you need to declare the entity that its results should map to. As simple as that.

Paging works the exact same way, in database-independent fashion by means of **SetMaxResults** and **SetFirstResult**:

```
//paging
var productsFrom10To20 = session.CreateSQLQuery("SELECT * FROM Product").Set
FirstResult(10)
.SetMaxResults(10).List();
```

 Note: NHibernate will properly make changes to your query such as wrapping it inside another query that does the paging.

Parameters are also used the same way (be sure to use them); however, always use ':' as the parameter prefix regardless of the database you are targeting:

```
//parameters
var productsWithPriceLowerThan100 = session.CreateSQLQuery(
"SELECT {p.*} FROM Product p WHERE p.price < :price").AddEntity("p", typeof(
Product))
.SetParameter("price", 100).List<Product>();
```

Multi Queries and Futures

For some databases that support it, such as SQL Server and Oracle, NHibernate offers a way to send multiple queries at the same time, thus avoiding multiple roundtrips. It is called multi queries and a simplified version is called futures. Let's see what they look like.

Multi queries can be used for the Criteria, Query Over, and HQL APIs. All of their usual options are supported including paging and parameters:

```
//HQL
IMultiQuery mq = session.CreateMultiQuery();
mq = mq.Add("from Product p where p.Price < :price").SetParameter("price", 1
0000);
mq = mq.Add("from Customer c");
mq = mq.Add("select distinct o.Date from Order o");

//queries are only sent to the database here
IList results = mq.List();

IEnumerable<Product> products = (results[0] as IList).OfType<Product>();
IEnumerable<Customer> customers = (results[1] as IList).OfType<Customer>();
IEnumerable<DateTime> dates = (results[2] as IList).OfType<DateTime>();
```

```
//Criteria
IMultiCriteria mc = session.CreateMultiCriteria();
mc = mc.Add(DetachedCriteria.For(typeof(Product)).Add(Restrictions.Lt(
Projections.Property("Price"), 10000)));
mc = mc.Add(session.QueryOver<Customer>());
mc = mc.Add(DetachedCriteria.For(typeof(Order)).SetProjection(Projections.Di
stinct(
Projections.Property("Date"))));

IList results = mc.List();

IEnumerable<Product> products = (results[0] as IList).OfType<Product>();
IEnumerable<Customer> customers = (results[1] as IList).OfType<Customer>();
IEnumerable<DateTime> dates = (results[2] as IList).OfType<DateTime>();
```

💡 *Tip: Beware! If you try to create a multi query on a database server that does not support it, NHibernate will throw an exception.*

Future queries and future values are similar to multi queries but operate on LINQ, Criteria, and Query Over queries:

```
//future queries
var futureProductsFromLinq = session.Query<Product>().ToFuture();
var futureFirstOrderFromHql = session.CreateQuery("from Order o order by o.D
ate desc take 1")
.Future<Order>();
var futureCustomersFromQueryOver = session.QueryOver<Customer>().Future();

//future single values
var futureProductsPriceSumFromCriteria = session.CreateCriteria(typeof(Produ
ct))
.SetProjection(Projections.Sum(Projections.Property("Price"))).FutureValue<D
ecimal>();

var futurePostsCountFromQueryOver = session.QueryOver<Post>().ToRowCountQuer
y()
.FutureValue<Int32>();

//query results - future queries are only sent to the database here
var products = futureProductsFromLinq.ToList();
var firstOrder = futureFirstOrderFromHql.Single();
var customers = futureCustomersFromQueryOver.ToList();

//single value results - future values are only sent to the database here
var postsCount = futurePostsCountFromQueryOver.Value;
var productsPriceSum = futureProductsPriceSumFromCriteria.Value;
```

💡 *Tip: If a given database engine does not support futures, it will silently ignore the future call and, instead, execute the query immediately. This is a big advantage of future queries.*

Lazy Loading

Because entities have references and collections of other entities, if NHibernate followed all these references, it could potentially load the entire database into memory! Just think about this for a moment:

1. You load a single **Blog**.
2. The **Blog** references a **User** and has a collection of **Posts**.
3. Each **Post** is associated with both a collection of **Comments** and **Attachments**.

As you can imagine, if NHibernate was to follow all of these associations, it would have to perform a lot of queries to retrieve all of the associated records from database and into memory. Depending on the use case, this may or may not be what you want. To help solve this problem, NHibernate offers lazy loading for both properties, references, and collections.

Lazy loading defers loading of records and columns until the properties that represent them are actually used by your code. For example:

- You have an **Order** with a lazy loaded **Customer**; this **Customer** won't be loaded at the time you load the **Order** but only when (and if) its **Customer** property is accessed.
- Your **Product** has a lazy loaded **Picture** property that represents it, and you don't always want the image loaded because it might potentially be very big.
- Your **Customer** has a lazy collection of **Orders**, and you seldom need to go through all of them.

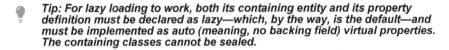 *Tip: For lazy loading to work, both its containing entity and its property definition must be declared as lazy—which, by the way, is the default—and must be implemented as auto (meaning, no backing field) virtual properties. The containing classes cannot be sealed.*

Remember the mappings from the other section? You can see there that for the **Blog** class, the class itself, the **Owner** property, and the **Posts** collections are all marked as lazy. In the **Post** class, it is also marked as lazy as are its **Attachments** and **Comments** collections.

Not all laziness is the same:

- An entity itself can be lazy loaded, which means that none of its columns are retrieved from the database. Instead, NHibernate returns a proxy object for representing the record, which will load it when any of its properties is accessed.
- For properties, you can only say that they are lazy or not.
- For associations, if you use the default **Proxy/proxy** setting, NHibernate will generate a proxy that inherits from the class declared in the property type. There will be a problem if this property type is the root class of a hierarchy because .NET does not have multiple inheritance. This is also because the proxy already inherits directly from the property's class; it won't be able to also inherit from the actual class that the association relates to. To avoid this problem, always specify the **NoProxy/no-proxy** setting; it will work for both class hierarchies as well as single classes. In this case, NHibernate will only assign a value to the property once it knows what class to create, so inheritance will be respected.

- As for collections, there are options for indexed and non-indexed ones. For non-indexed collections, including collections of values, sets, and bags, the only option we have for them is to either be lazy (meaning, load all of the collection entities only when the collection is accessed) or not lazy (load all collection entities when its root entity is loaded). But, for indexed collections (lists, maps), we have a third option: **ExtraLazy/extra**. This tells NHibernate to only load each collection item as it is accessed, not all at the same time. Finally, array collections cannot be lazy loaded.

 Note: A lazy property, association or collection will only be fetched from the database one time, when it is accessed. After that, it will be stored in memory. If an entity has several lazy properties—not associations or collections—all of them will be loaded at the same time. This is different from what happens for associations and collections.

So, to sum it all up:

Laziness Options

Member Type	Member Subtype	Laziness Options
Properties (including components)	N/A	**True**, **False**
References	N/A	**Proxy**, **NoProxy**, **NoLazy**
Collections	Indexed (list, map)	**Lazy**, **NoLazy**, **Extra**
	Non-indexed (set, bag)	**Lazy**, **NoLazy**
	Arrays (array, primitive array)	N/A

When will you use lazy loading? Probably most of the time—at least for references and collections. You won't need it when you are certain that after you load an entity you will go through some of its references and collections. When this happens, you might as well specify the **Join/join** fetch strategy; this will bring everything in a single SELECT instead of a SELECT for the root entity and one SELECT for each association or collection (the default strategy). Here's how it is declared in XML:

```xml
<?xml version="1.0" encoding="utf-8"?>
<hibernate-mapping namespace="Succinctly.Model" assembly="Succinctly.Model"
xmlns="urn:nhibernate-mapping-2.2">
  <class name="Post" lazy="true" table="`POST`">
    <!-- ... -->
    <many-to-one name="Blog" column="`BLOG_ID`" not-
null="true" lazy="false" fetch="join" />
```

```
    </class>
</hibernate-mapping>
```

An in-mapping by code:

```
mapper.Class<Blog>(ca =>
{
  //...
  ca.ManyToOne(c => c.Owner, a =>
  {
    //...
    a.Fetch(FetchKind.Join);
    a.Lazy(LazyRelation.NoLazy);
  });
  ca.List(x => x.Posts, x =>
  {
    //...
    x.Fetch(CollectionFetchMode.Join);
    x.Lazy(CollectionLazy.NoLazy);
  }, c => c.OneToMany());
});
```

> 💡 ***Tip: Specifying the fetch strategy as*** *Join* ***only has meaning if lazy loading is not used. Also, disabling lazy loading and using*** *Select* ***for fetching is pointless, too.***

Lazy loading by id is achieved by calling the **Load** method on a lazy-loadable entity:

```
//get strongly typed (possibly) proxy by id
var someBlogProxy = session.Load<Blog>(1);

//get object (possibly) proxy by id and type
var someObjectProxy = session.Load(typeof(Blog), 1);
```

What this does is:

- If the referenced entity was already loaded by the current session, no proxy will be returned but the entity itself.
- If the entity isn't known by the current session, a proxy will be returned. The database won't be touched until code accesses some property of this entity (except the id property).
- If no record exists for the given primary key, a proxy will still be returned. Remember, it doesn't access the database. In this case, when a property is accessed, it will throw an exception because, at that point, it will try to fetch the record from the database but it doesn't exist.
- If a record does exist for the given identifier, when some property is touched, the entity will be populated from the record's columns.

> ***Note: If an instance pointing to the same record is already present in the session's cache, it will be returned instead of a proxy.***

LINQ and HQL queries always treat associations and collections as lazy so, if you want them to come at the same time as their containers, you have to fetch them explicitly. This can even be done for multiple levels:

```
//fetching multiple levels in HQL
var blogs = session.CreateQuery("from Blog b join fetch b.Posts p join fetch
  p.Comments")
.List<Blog>();

//fetching multiple levels in LINQ
var blogs = session.Query<Blog>().FetchMany(x => x.Posts).ThenFetch(x => x.C
omments).ToList();

//fetching a single level in Criteria
var blogs = session.CreateCriteria(typeof(Blog)).SetFetchMode("Posts", Fetch
Mode.Eager)
.List<Blog>();

//fetching a single level in Query Over
var blogs = session.QueryOver<Blog>().Fetch(x => x.Posts).Eager.List();
```

You can check if a property, reference or collection is already loaded without actually loading it:

```
//load an entity
Blog o = session.Get<Blog>(1);
Boolean isCustomerInitialized = NHibernateUtil.IsPropertyInitialized(o, "Own
er");
```

Finally, a word of caution: Lazy loading requires the originating session to be available so that NHibernate can go to the database when necessary. If you have disposed of the session, you will get a runtime exception. This is particularly relevant if you have entity instances that span multiple NHibernate sessions. Think of entities stored in an ASP.NET session, for instance. In this case, make sure you explicitly load everything you need before the session goes away.

 Note: If you won't be using lazy loading, you don't need to mark properties and methods as virtual, and you can have sealed classes.

Inheritance

We saw earlier the ways by which we can store our inheritance model in the database. For querying, we can also both look explicitly for entities of a concrete type or for all entities of a base class, using any of the querying APIs regardless of the actual inheritance strategy. Some examples follow:

```
//query from a base class
var personById = session.Get<Person>(1);
var personById = session.Get(typeof(Person), 1);
var allPeopleFromLinq = session.Query<Person>().ToList();
```

```
var allPeopleFromHql = session.CreateQuery("from Person").List<Person>();
var allPeopleFromCriteria = session.CreateCriteria(typeof(Person)).List<Pers
on>();
var allPeopleFromQueryOver = session.QueryOver<Person>().List<Person>();

//query a derived class
var nationalCitizensFromLinq = session.Query<NationalCitizen>().ToList();

var foreignCitizensFromLinq = session.Query<Person>().Where(x => x is Foreig
nCitizen)
.Cast<ForeignCitizen>().ToList();

var nationalCitizenFromCriteria = session.CreateCriteria(typeof(Person), "p"
)
.Add(Property.ForName("p.class").Eq(typeof(NationalCitizen))).List<NationalC
itizen>();

var nationalCitizenFromQueryOver = session.QueryOver<Person>()
.Where(x => x.GetType() == typeof(NationalCitizen)).List<NationalCitizen>();

var nationalCitizensFromHql = session
.CreateQuery("from Person p where p.class = Succinctly.Model.NationalCitizen
")
.List<NationalCitizen>();

var foreignCitizensFromHql = session.CreateQuery("from ForeignCitizen")
.List<ForeignCitizen>();
```

Tip: The class *pseudo-property can only be used when we are querying a class hierarchy; otherwise, it is useless and will cause an error.*

Refreshing

After an entity is loaded, it is stored in the first-level cache of the session. This means that whenever the same record is loaded by some query, NHibernate doesn't need to create a new instance for it; instead it can return the existing entity. This raises a question: What if the record was changed after it was first loaded? To get the most recent values, we use the **Refresh** method of the **ISession**:

```
Blog b = session.Get<Blog>(1);
//...
session.Refresh(b);
```

This will issue a SELECT statement and the entity instance will have its properties loaded once again.

Which One Shall I Choose?

The one you choose depends on what you want to do. A few tips:

- LINQ is great due to its SQL-like syntax and because it is now ubiquitous in .NET as a generic, data source-independent querying API.
- LINQ and Query Over are good because they are both strongly typed, and therefore refactor-friendly.
- Criteria and HQL are good for dynamic query construction and because they can be used to query even non-public properties.
- Criteria, Query Over, and HQL can be used to express functions and expressions (think of LIKE, for example) that cannot be expressed in LINQ.
- SQL offers all the power of the database.

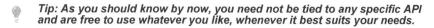 *Tip: As you should know by now, you need not be tied to any specific API and are free to use whatever you like, whenever it best suits your needs.*

Chapter 6 Making Changes

Inserting, Updating, and Deleting

Besides querying, you will also want to make changes. Because NHibernate uses POCOs to represent records in a database, when you need to insert a new record, you start by creating a new instance of a mapped class:

```
Product p = new Product() { Name = "NHibernate Succinctly", Price = 0 };
```

Then, you tell NHibernate to persist it:

```
session.Save(p);
```

If you have associations that you wish to store along with the root aggregate, you must get a reference to them first:

```
Post post = new Post();
post.Blog = session.Get<Post>(1);
```

In this type of association, what really matters is the foreign key; you might as well load a proxy instead, which has the advantage of not actually going to the database:

```
//or get a proxy, no need to go to the database if we only need the foreign
key
post.Blog = session.Load<Post>(1);
```

In this case, however, if the referenced entity does not exist, an exception will be thrown when NHibernate attempts to save the root aggregate.

In the case of bidirectional associations, it is recommended that you fill both sides of the relationship if you are going to work with the entities immediately, for coherence:

```
Post post = new Post();
post.Blog = session.Get<Blog>(1);
post.Blog.Posts.Add(post);
```

For your convenience, you can add a simple method to the Blog class for hooking the two endpoints:

```
public void AddPost(Post post)
{
  post.Blog = this;
  this.Posts.Add(post);
}
```

Depending on your session configuration, this may or not be all that it takes. (More on this in the next section, Flushing Changes.)

NHibernate implements something called first-level cache in its **ISession**. What this means is, all of the entities that it loads or are marked for saving are stored in a memory cache. For each of these entities, when it is loaded, NHibernate takes a snapshot of its initial state and stores it internally. When it is time for persisting changes to the database, NHibernate will check all of the entities present in its first-level cache for the current values of their properties and will detect those entities whose properties have changed. This is called change tracking, and such entities are said to be dirty. A dirty session contains at least one dirty entity.

Because change tracking is automatic, there is normally no need to explicitly update an entity. However, the **ISession** has an **Update** method that you can call to force an update:

```
session.Update(p);
```

And, if you need to delete an entity from the database, you call the session's **Delete** method upon this entity:

```
session.Delete(p);
```

Finally, when you have an entity with a loaded collection (a one-to-many or many-to-many) and you want to remove all of its elements, instead of iterating one by one and calling **Delete**, you can just call **Clear** on the collection property:

```
Blog blog = session.Get<Blog>(1);
blog.Posts.Clear();
```

NHibernate will then issue a single DELETE statement for all of the child records.

Pay attention: You can only call **Delete** on a tracked entity; that is, one that was either loaded from the database or explicitly added to it, by calling **Save**. After you do it, you should no longer access this entity instance because nothing you can do with it will prevent it from being deleted.

NHibernate will store, update or delete each entity in the database by issuing appropriate SQL commands whenever the session is flushed. In a nutshell, what this means is:

- New entities need to be marked explicitly for saving, by calling **Save**.
- Existing tracked entities will detect changes made upon them automatically. There is no need to explicitly mark them for updating; that is, no need to call any method.
- If you are not sure if an entity was already saved, you can call **SaveOrUpdate**.
- You delete a tracked entity by calling **Delete** explicitly on it.

Flushing Changes

When does NHibernate know that it is time to persist all changes from the first-level cache to the database (in other words, flush)? It depends on the flush mode (the **FlushMode** property) of the current **ISession**. It is the **FlushMode** that controls when it happens. The possible options are:

- **Always**: NHibernate will persist dirty entities before issuing any query and immediately after the **Save** or **Delete** methods are called.
- **Auto**: NHibernate will send changes to the database if a query is being issued for some entity and there are dirty entities of the same type.
- **Commit**: Flushing will only occur when the current transaction is committed.
- **Never**: You need to call **Flush** explicitly on the current **ISession**.
- **Unspecified**: The default, identical to **Auto**.

Some notes:

- You should generally avoid **Always** as it may slow down NHibernate because it will need to check the first-level cache before issuing any query.
- **Never** is also something to avoid because it is possible that you could forget to call **Flush** and all changes will be lost.
- **Commit** and **Auto** are okay. **Commit** is even better because it forces you to use transactions (which is a best practice).

Updating Disconnected Entities

What happens if you have an entity that was loaded in a different session and you want to be able to change or delete it in another session? This other session does not know anything about this entity; it is not in its first-level cache and so, from its point of view, it is an untracked or disconnected entity.

You have two options:

1. Update the memory entity with the current values for its associated record in the database and then apply changes:

```
Product product;

using (ISession session = sessionFactory.OpenSession())
{
    //load some entity and store it somewhere with a greater scope than this
session
    product = session.Query<Product>().First();
}

using (ISession session = sessionFactory.OpenSession())
{
    //retrieve current values from the database before making changes
    product = session.Merge<Product>(product);
    product.Price = 10;
    session.Flush();
}
```

2. Force the current values of the entity to be persisted, ignoring the current values in the database:

```
using (ISession session = sessionFactory.OpenSession())
{
```

```
//save current entity properties to the database without an additional
select
  product.Price = 10;
  session.SaveOrUpdateCopy(product);
  session.Flush();
}
```

Removing from the First-Level Cache

Long-lived NHibernate sessions will typically end up with many entities to track—those loaded from queries. This may eventually cause performance problems because, when the time comes for flushing, the session has a lot of instances and values to check for dirtiness.

When you no longer need to track an entity, you can call **ISession.Evict** to remove it from cache:

```
session.Evict(product);
```

Or, you can clear the entire session:

```
session.Clear();
```

 Tip: This will lose all tracked entities as well as any changes they might have, so use with caution.

Another option would be to mark the entity as read-only, which means its state won't be looked at when the session is flushed:

```
session.SetReadOnly(product, true);
```

 Note: At any later stage, if the entity is still being tracked, you can always revert it by calling SetReadOnly again with a false parameter.

Executable HQL

NHibernate also supports bulk DML operations by using the HQL API. This is called executable HQL and inserts, updates, and deletes are supported:

```
//unconditional update
Int32 updatedRecords = session.CreateQuery("update Product p set p.Price = p
.Price * 2")
.ExecuteUpdate();

//delete with parameter
```

```
Int32 deletedRecords = session.CreateQuery("delete from Product p where p.Pr
ice = :price")
.SetParameter("price", 0).ExecuteUpdate();
//delete from query
Int32 deletedRecords = session.Delete("from Product p where p.Price = 0");

//insert based on existing records
Int32 insertedRecords = session.CreateQuery(
"insert into Product (ProductId, Name, Price, Specification) select p.Produc
tId * 10, p.Name + ' copy', p.Price * 2, p.Specification from Product p").Ex
ecuteUpdate();
```

NHibernate will not make changes to entities that exist in the first-level cache; that is, if you have loaded an entity and then either modify or delete it by using HQL. This entity will not know anything about it. If you have deleted it with HQL and you try to save it later, an error will occur because there is no record to update.

Pay attention to this: You normally don't have to think about identifier generation patterns. But, if you are going to insert records by using HQL and you don't use the IDENTITY generation pattern, you need to generate the ids yourself. In this example, we are creating them from entries that already exist because you can only insert in HQL from records returned from a **select**.

Detecting Changes

The **IsDirty** property of the **ISession** will tell you if there are either new entities marked for saving, entities marked for deletion, or loaded entities that have changed values for some of their properties—as compared to the ones they had when loaded from the database.

You can examine entities in the first-level cache yourself by using the NHibernate API:

```
//enumerate all entities in the first level cache
public static IEnumerable<T> Local<T>(this ISession session, Status status =
Status.Loaded)
{
  var impl = session.GetSessionImplementation();
  var pc = impl.PersistenceContext;

  foreach (T key in pc.EntityEntries.Keys.OfType<T>())
  {
    var entry = pc.EntityEntries[key] as EntityEntry;

    if (entry.Status == status)
    {
      yield return (key);
    }
  }
}
```

This extension method may come in handy if you have loaded a lot of entities and you need to find a particular one. You can look it up in the first-level cache first before going to the database. Or you can find entities with a particular state such as **Deleted**, for instance.

Because NHibernate stores the original values for all mapped properties of an entity, you can look at them to see what has changed:

```
//find dirty properties for a loaded entity
public static Dictionary<String, Object> GetDirtyProperties<T>(this ISession
  session, T entity)
{
    var sessionImpl = session.GetSessionImplementation();
    var context = sessionImpl.PersistenceContext;
    var entry = context.GetEntry(context.Unproxy(entity));

    if ((entry == null) ||
(entry.RequiresDirtyCheck(entity) == false) || (entry.ExistsInDatabase == fa
lse)
    || (entry.LoadedState == null))
    {
      //entity does not exist in the first level cache
      return (null);
    }

    var persister = entry.Persister;
    var propertyNames = persister.PropertyNames;

var currentState = persister.GetPropertyValues(entity, sessionImpl.EntityMod
e);
    var loadedState = entry.LoadedState;
    var dp = (persister.EntityMetamodel.Properties
.Where((property, i) => (LazyPropertyInitializer.UnfetchedProperty.Equals(lo
adedState[i]) ==
false) && (property.Type.IsDirty(loadedState[i], currentState[i], sessionImp
l) == true)))
.ToArray();

    return

(dp.ToDictionary(x => x.Name, x => currentState[Array.IndexOf(propertyNames,
  x.Name)]));
}
```

Cascading Changes

Entities with references to other entities, either direct references (a property of the type of another entity) or collections can propagate changes made to themselves to these references. The most obvious cases are:

- When a root entity is saved, save all of its references if they are not already saved (insert records in the corresponding tables).

- When a parent entity is deleted, delete all of its child entities (delete records from the child tables that referenced the parent record).
- When an entity that is referenced by other entities is deleted, remove its reference from all of these entities (set the foreign key to the main record to **NULL**).

In NHibernate's terms, this is called cascading. Cascade supports the following options which may be specified either in mapping by code, XML or attributes:

- **Detach/evict**: The child entity is removed (evicted) from the session when its parent is also evicted, usually by calling **ISession.Evict**.
- **Merge/merge**: When a parent entity is merged into the current session, usually by **ISession.Merge**, children are also merged.
- **Persist/save-update**: When a root entity is about to be saved or updated, its children are also saved or updated.
- **ReAttach/lock**: When a parent entity is locked, also lock its children.
- **Refresh/refresh**: When a parent entity is refreshed, also refresh its children.
- **Remove/delete**: Deletes the child entity when its parent is deleted.
- **None/none**: Do nothing, this is the default.
- **All/all**: The same as **Persist** and **Remove**; all child entities that are not saved are saved, and if the parent is deleted, they are also deleted.
- **DeleteOrphans/delete-orphan**: if a child entity of a one-to-many relation no longer references the original parent entity, or any other, remove it from the database.
- **All** and **DeleteOrphans/all-delete-orphan**: the combined behavior of **All** and **DeleteOrphans**.

Cascading can be tricky. Some general guidelines:

- For entities that depend on the existence of another entity, use **DeleteOrphans** because, if the relation is broken (you set the property to null), the entity cannot exist by itself and must be removed.
- For collections, you normally would use **All** (possibly together with **DeleteOrphans**). If you want all of the entities in the collection to be saved and deleted whenever their parent is, or use **Persist** if you don't want them to be deleted with their parent but want them to be saved automatically.
- For many-to-one references you normally won't want **Delete** because usually the referenced entity should live longer than the entities that reference it; use **Persist** instead.

To apply cascading by code, use this example (same mapping as in section Mapping by Code):

```
public class BlogMapping : ClassMapping<Blog>
{
  public BlogMapping()
  {
    //...
    this.ManyToOne(x => x.Owner, x =>
    {
      x.Cascade(Cascade.Persist);
      //...
    });
    this.List(x => x.Posts, x =>
```

```csharp
        {
            //...
            x.Cascade(Cascade.All | Cascade.DeleteOrphans);
        }, x =>
        {
            //...
        });
    }
}

public class PostMapping : ClassMapping<Post>
{
    //...
    this.Set(x => x.Tags, x =>
    {
        //...
        x.Cascade(Cascade.All);
    }, x =>
    {
        //...
    });
    this.Set(x => x.Attachments, x =>
    {
        //...
        x.Cascade(Cascade.All | Cascade.DeleteOrphans);
    }, x =>
    {
        //...
    });
    this.Bag(x => x.Comments, x =>
    {
        //...
        x.Cascade(Cascade.All | Cascade.DeleteOrphans);
    }, x =>
    {
        //...
    });
}
```

With XML, it would look like this (again, same mapping as in XML Mappings):

```xml
<hibernate-mapping namespace="Succinctly.Model" assembly="Succinctly.Model"
xmlns="urn:nhibernate-mapping-2.2">
  <class name="Blog" lazy="true" table="`BLOG`">
    <!-- ... -->
    <many-to-one name="Owner" column="`USER_ID`" not-null="true" lazy="no-
proxy"
cascade="save-update"/>
    <list cascade="all-delete-
orphan" inverse="true" lazy="true" name="Posts">
      <!-- ... -->
    </list>
  </class>
</hibernate-mapping>

<hibernate-mapping namespace="Succinctly.Model" assembly="Succinctly.Model"
```

```
xmlns="urn:nhibernate-mapping-2.2">
  <class name="Post" lazy="true" table="`POST`">
    <!-- ... -->
    <set cascade="all" lazy="false" name="Tags" table="`TAG`" order-
by="`TAG`">
      <!-- ... -->
    </set>
    <set cascade="all-delete-
orphan" inverse="true" lazy="true" name="Attachments">
      <!-- ... -->
    </set>
    <bag cascade="all-delete-
orphan" inverse="true" lazy="true" name="Comments">
      <!-- ... -->
    </bag>
  </class>
</hibernate-mapping>
```

And finally, with attributes (see Mapping by Attributes for the full mapping):

```
public class Blog
{
  //...
[ManyToOne(0, Column = "user_id", NotNull = true, Lazy = Laziness.NoProxy, N
ame = "Owner",
Cascade = "save-update")]
  public virtual User Owner { get; set; }
  //...
  [List(0, Cascade = "all-delete-
orphan", Lazy = CollectionLazy.True, Inverse = true, Generic = true)]
  public virtual IList<Post> Posts { get; protected set; }
}

public class Post
{

[Set(0, Name = "Tags", Table = "tag", OrderBy = "tag", Lazy = CollectionLazy
.False, Cascade = "all"
, Generic = true)]
  public virtual Iesi.Collections.Generic.ISet<String> Tags { get;
protected set; }
  [Set(0, Name = "Attachments", Inverse = true, Lazy = CollectionLazy.True,
Cascade = "all-delete-orphan", Generic = true)]
  public virtual Iesi.Collections.Generic.ISet<Attachment> Attachments {
get; protected set; }

[Bag(0, Name = "Comments", Inverse = true, Lazy = CollectionLazy.True, Gener
ic = true,
Cascade = "all-delete-orphan")]
  public virtual IList<Comment> Comments { get; protected set; }
}
```

An example is in order. Imagine that your entities are not using cascade and you have to save everything by hand:

```
Blog b = new Blog() { Creation = new DateTime(2008, 8, 13), Name = "Developm
ent With A Dot" };
b.Owner = new User() { Birthday = new DateTime(1975, 8, 19), Username = "ric
ardoperes" };
b.Posts.Add(new Post() { Blog = b, Content = "Some Post", Title = "Some Titl
e", Timestamp = DateTime.Now });

session.Save(b.Owner);
session.Save(b);
session.Save(b.Posts.First());
session.Flush();
```

Whereas, if you have cascading set for the **Owner** and **Posts** properties of the **Blog** class, you only need to call **Save** once, for the root **Blog** instance, because all of the other entities are accessible (and cascaded) from it:

```
session.Save(b);
session.Flush();
```

Should you ever need to delete a **Blog** instance, all of its **Posts**, related **Comments** and **Attachments** will be deleted at the same time but not its **Owner**.

```
session.Delete(b);
session.Flush();
```

Transactions

As you know, when changing multiple records at the same time, especially if one change depends on the other, we need to use transactions. All relational databases support transactions, and so does NHibernate.

Transactions in NHibernate come in two flavors:

- NHibernate-specific transactions, which are useful when they are clearly delimited; that is, we know when they should start and terminate and should only affect NHibernate operations.
- .NET ambient transactions, for when we have to coordinate access to multiple databases simultaneously or enlist in existing transactions that may even be distributed.

With NHibernate, you really should have a transaction whenever you may be making changes to a database. Remember that not all changes are explicit. For example, a change in a loaded entity may cause it to be updated on the database. If you use transactions, you won't have any bad experiences. Whenever you use transactions, set the flush mode of the session to the appropriate value:

```
session.FlushMode = FlushMode.Commit;
```

This will cause NHibernate to only send changes to the database when (and only if) the current transaction is committed.

The transaction API can be used like this:

```
using (ISession session = sessionFactory.OpenSession())
using (ITransaction tx = session.BeginTransaction())
{
  session.FlushMode = FlushMode.Commit;

  //make changes

  if (/* if everything is OK, commit */)
  {
    tx.Commit();
  }
  else
  {
    //otherwise, rollback (which is also done automatically if Commit is not
called)
    tx.Rollback();
  }
}
```

All operations performed on an **ISession** instance that is running under a transaction are automatically enlisted in it; this includes explicit saves, updates and deletes, automatic updates due to dirty properties, custom SQL commands, and executable HQL queries.

You can check the current state of a transaction and even check if one was started:

```
//the Transaction property of the ISession holds the current
transaction
Boolean transactionActive = session.Transaction.IsActive;

Boolean committed = tx.WasCommitted;
Boolean rolledback = session.Transaction.WasRolledBack;
```

The alternative to this API is **System.Transactions**, .NET's standard transaction API:

```
using (TransactionScope tx = new TransactionScope())
{
  using (ISession session1 = sessionFactory1.OpenSession())
  {
    session1.FlushMode = FlushMode.Commit;

    Product p = new Product() { Name = "A
Name", Price = 5, Specification = XDocument.Parse("<data/>") };

    session1.Save(p);
  }

  using (ISession session2 = sessionFactory2.OpenSession())
  {
    session2.FlushMode = FlushMode.Commit;
```

```
    Product p = session2.Query<Product>().Where(x => x.Name == "Another
Name").Single();

    session2.Delete(p);
}

//there is no Rollback method, if Complete is not called, the transaction
is rolled back
    tx.Complete();
}
```

Both NHibernate and System transactions allow specifying the isolation level:

```
ITransaction tx = session.BeginTransaction(System.Data.IsolationLevel.Serial
izable);

new TransactionScope(TransactionScopeOption.Required, new TransactionOptions
() {
IsolationLevel = System.Transactions.IsolationLevel.Serializable });
```

Just remember this:

- Use them at all times!
- Either with NHibernate or System transactions, always create them in a **using** block so that they are automatically disposed.
- Set the session's flush mode to **Commit** to avoid unnecessary trips to the database.
- Make sure you call **Commit** (on NHibernate transactions) or **Complete** (on System ones) when you are done with the changes and you want to make them permanent.
- If you are going to access multiple databases simultaneously in a System transaction, you must start the **Distributed Transaction Coordinator** service or else you may get unexpected exceptions when you access the second database:

Figure 26: Distributed Transaction Coordinator Service

Pessimistic Locking

At times, there may be a need to lock one or more records in a table so that nobody else can make modifications to them behind our back. This is called concurrency control. Different databases use different mechanisms for this but NHibernate offers an independent API. Locking involves a lock mode, for which the following values exist:

Mode	Description
Force	Similar to **Upgrade** but causes a version increment, if the entity is versioned
None	Not used
Read	When an entity is read without specifying a **LockMode**
Upgrade	Switch from not locked to locked; if the record is already locked, will wait for the other lock to be released
UpgradeNoWait	Same as **Upgrade** but, in case the record is already locked, will return immediately instead of waiting for the other lock to be released (but the lock mode will remain the same)
Write	When an entity was inserted from the current session

Locking must always be called in the context of a transaction. NHibernate always synchronizes the lock mode of a record in the database with its in-memory (first-level cache) representation.

For locking a single record upon loading, we can pass an additional parameter to the **Get** method:

```
Product p = session.Get<Product>(1, LockMode.Upgrade);
```

Which will result in the following SQL in SQL Server:

```
SELECT
    product0_.product_id,
    product0_.name,
    product0_.specification,
    product0_.price
FROM
    product product0_
WITH (UPDLOCK, ROWLOCK)
WHERE
```

```
    product0_.product_id = 1
```

But we can also lock a record after loading:

```
session.Lock(p, LockMode.Upgrade);
```

And it will result in this SQL being sent (notice that it is not bringing the columns):

```
SELECT
    product0_.product_id,
FROM
    product product0_
WITH (UPDLOCK, ROWLOCK)
WHERE
    product0_.product_id = 1
```

And locking the results of a query (HQL, Criteria, and Query Over) is possible, too:

```
//hql
session.CreateQuery("from Product p").SetLockMode("p", LockMode.Upgrade);

//criteria
session.CreateCriteria(typeof(Product)).SetLockMode(LockMode.Upgrade).List<Product>();

//query over
session.QueryOver<Product>().Lock().Upgrade.List();
```

For getting the lock state of a record:

```
LockMode mode = session.GetCurrentLockMode(p);
```

Whenever the lock mode is **Upgrade**, **UpgradeNoWait**, **Write** or **Force**, you know the record is being locked by the current session.

 Tip: Generally speaking, locking at the record level is not scalable and is not very useful in the context of web applications which are, by nature, disconnected and stateless. So you should generally avoid it in favor of optimistic locking (coming up next). At the very least, do limit the number of records you lock to the very minimum amount possible.

Optimistic Concurrency

Optimistic concurrency is a process for handling concurrency which doesn't involve locking. With optimistic locking, we assume that no one is locking the record and we can compare all or some of the previously loaded record's values with the values currently in the database to see if something has changed (when an UPDATE is issued). If the UPDATE affects no records, we know that something indeed has changed.

NHibernate offers several optimistic concurrency possibilities:

- None: No optimistic locking will be processed, usually known as "last one wins." This is the default.
- Dirty: All dirty (meaning, changed) mapped properties are compared with their current values in the database.
- All: All mutable mapped properties are compared with the current values.
- Versioned: One column of the table is used for comparison.

When we use versioning, we also have several strategies for obtaining and updating the version column:

- Using a database-specific mechanism such as SQL Server's **TIMESTAMP/ROWVERSION** (http://msdn.microsoft.com/en-us/library/ms182776.aspx) or Oracle's **ORA_ROWSCN** (http://docs.oracle.com/cd/B19306_01/server.102/b14200/pseudocolumns007.htm); this requires no work from NHibernate other than loading the current value.
- Using an integer number for the version which NHibernate must update explicitly.
- Using a date and time which can either be obtained from the database or from .NET which NHibernate is also responsible for updating.

No strategy is the default. If we want to have **Dirty** or **All**, we need to configure it on an entity-by-entity basis.

In XML:

```
<hibernate-mapping namespace="Succinctly.Model" assembly="Succinctly.Model"
xmlns="urn:nhibernate-mapping-2.2">
  <class name="Blog" lazy="true" table="`BLOG`" optimistic-lock="dirty"
dynamic-update="true">
    <!-- ... -->
  </class>
</hibernate-mapping>
```

And attributes:

```
[Class(Table = "blog", Lazy = true, OptimisticLock = OptimisticLockMode.Dirt
y, DynamicUpdate = true)]
public class Blog
{
    //...
}
```

Unfortunately, as of now, mapping by code does not allow setting the optimistic lock mode. But you can still achieve it by code on the **Configuration** instance:

```
cfg.GetClassMapping(typeof(Blog)).OptimisticLockMode = Versioning.Optimistic
Lock.Dirty;
cfg.GetClassMapping(typeof(Blog)).DynamicUpdate = true;
```

In this case, a change to a property in a **Product** instance would lead to the following SQL being issued (in real life, with parameters instead of numbers):

```
UPDATE product
SET price = 10
WHERE product_id = 1
AND price = 5
```

As you can see, the "`price = 5`" condition is not strictly required but NHibernate is sending it because of the optimistic lock mode of **Dirty** and because the **Price** property was changed.

Like I said, instead of **Dirty**, you can use **All**. In either case, you must also add the **dynamic-update** attribute; it is a requirement. And what it means is, instead of issuing a SET for each of the mapped columns, it will only issue one for the columns whose values have changed. You need not worry about it; no additional columns in the database or properties in the model need to be added.

For the same updated **Product** instance, when using **All** as the optimistic lock mode, the SQL would be:

```
UPDATE product
SET price = 10
WHERE product_id = 1
AND price = 5
AND specification = /* ... */
AND picture = /* ... */
```

As you can see, in this case all columns are compared, which may be slightly slower.

As for versioned columns, we need to add a new property to our entity for storing the original version. Its type depends on what mechanism we want to use. For example, if we want to use SQL Server's **ROWVERSION**, we would have a property defined like this:

```
public virtual Byte[] Version { get; protected set; }
```

And we would map it by code, like this (in a **ClassMapping<T>** or **ModelMapper** class):

```
this.Version(x => x.Version, x =>
{
  x.Column(y =>
  {
    y.NotNullable(true);
    y.Name("version");
    y.SqlType("ROWVERSION");
```

```
    });
    x.Insert(false);
    x.Generated(VersionGeneration.Always);
    x.Type(NHibernateUtil.BinaryBlob as IVersionType);
});
```

We have to tell NHibernate to always have the database generate the version for us, to not insert the value when it is inserting a record for our entity, to use the SQL type **ROWVERSION** when creating a table for the entity, and to use the NHibernate **BinaryBlobType**, a type that allows versioning, for handling data for this column.

With attributes, this is how it would look:

```
[Version(0, Name =
"Version", Column = "version", Generated = VersionGeneration.Always, Insert
= false,
TypeType = typeof(BinaryBlobType))]
[Column(1, SqlType = "ROWVERSION")]
public virtual Byte[] Version { get; protected set; }
```

And finally, in XML:

```
<class name="Product" lazy="true" table="`product`">
    <!-- ... --
><version name="Version" column="version" generated="always" insert="false"
type="BinaryBlob"/>
    <!-- ... -->
</class>
```

Whereas, for Oracle's **ORA_ROWSCN**, the property declaration would be instead:

```
public virtual Int64[] Version { get; protected set; }
```

And its fluent mappings:

```
this.Version(x => x.Version, x =>
{
    x.Column(y =>
    {
        y.NotNullable(true);
        y.Name("ora_rowscn");
    });
    x.Insert(false);
    x.Generated(VersionGeneration.Always);
});
```

Attribute mappings:

```
[Version(Name =
"Version", Column = "ora_rowscn", Generated = VersionGeneration.Always, Inse
rt = false)]
public virtual Int64[] Version { get; protected set; }
```

And, finally, XML:

```xml
<class name="Product" lazy="true" table="`product`">
  <!-- ... -->

<version name="Version" column="ora_rowscn" generated="always" insert="false
" />
  <!-- ... -->
</class>
```

Database-specific strategies are great because they leverage each database's optimized mechanisms, and version columns are automatically updated. But they render our code less portable and require an additional SELECT after each UPDATE in order to find out what value the record has.

For database-independent strategies, we can choose either a number or a date/time as the version column. For a number (the default versioning strategy), we add an integer property to our class:

```csharp
public virtual Int32[] Version { get; protected set; }
```

And we map it by code:

```csharp
this.Version(x => x.Version, x =>
{
  x.Column(y =>
  {
    y.NotNullable(true);
    y.Name("version");
  });
});
```

By XML:

```xml
<class name="Product" lazy="true" table="`product`">
  <!-- ... -->
  <version name="Version" column="version" />
  <!-- ... -->
</class>
```

Or by attributes:

```csharp
[Version(Name = "Version", Column = "version")]
public virtual Int32[] Version { get; protected set; }
```

If we instead want to use a date/time, we need to add a type attribute and change the property's type:

```csharp
public virtual DateTime[] Version { get; protected set; }
```

And we need to update the mapping to use a **TimestampType**:

```
this.Version(x => x.Version, x =>
{
  x.Column(y =>
  {
    y.NotNullable(true);
    y.Name("version");
  });
  x.Type(NHibernateUtil.Timestamp as IVersionType);
});
```

By XML:

```
<class name="Product" lazy="true" table="`product`">
  <!-- ... -->
  <version name="Version" column="version" type="timestamp"/>
  <!-- ... -->
</class>
```

And attributes:

```
[Version(Name =
"Version", Column = "version", TypeType = typeof(TimestampType))]
public virtual DateTime[] Version { get; protected set; }
```

Once you update an optimistic locking strategy, your UPDATE SQL will look like this (with parameters instead of literals, of course):

```
UPDATE product
SET price = 10, version = 2
WHERE product_id = 1
AND version = 1
```

Generally speaking, whenever we update an entity, its version will increase, or in the case of date and time properties, will be set as the current timestamp. But we can specify on a property-by-property basis if changes made upon them should be considered when incrementing the version of the entity. This is achieved by the property's **optimistic lock** attribute as you can see in XML:

```
<property name="Timestamp" column="`TIMESTAMP`" not-null="true" optimistic-
lock="false" />
```

Code:

```
this.Property(x => x.Timestamp, x =>
{
  x.Column("timestamp");
  x.NotNullable(true);
  x.OptimisticLock(false);
});
```

And attributes mapping:

```
[Property(Name = "Timestamp", Column = "timestamp", NotNull = true, Optimist
icLock = false)]
public virtual DateTime Timestamp { get; set; }
```

Whenever the number of updated records is not what NHibernate expects, due to optimistic concurrency checks, NHibernate will throw a **StaleStateException**. When this happens, you have no alternative but to refresh the entity and try again.

Optimistic locking is very important when we may have multiple, simultaneous accesses to database tables and when explicit locking is impractical. For example, with web applications. After you map some entity using optimistic locking, its usage is transparent. If, however, you run into a situation in which the data on the database does not correspond to the data that was loaded for some entity, NHibernate will throw an exception when NHibernate flushes it.

As for its many options, I leave you with some tips:

- In general, avoid database-specific strategies, as they are less portable and have worse performance.
- Use **Dirty** or **All** optimistic locking modes when you do not need a column that stores the actual version.
- Use date/time versions when knowing the time of the record's last UPDATE is important to you and you don't mind adding an additional column to a table.
- Finally, choose numeric versioning as the most standard case.

When using Another option would be to mark the entity as read-only, which means its state won't be looked at when the session is flushed:

```
session.SetReadOnly(product, true);
```

 Note: At any later stage, if the entity is still being tracked, you can always revert it by calling SetReadOnly **again with a** false **parameter.**

Executable HQL for updating records, you can use the following syntax for updating version columns automatically, regardless of the actual strategy:

```
Int32 updatedRecords = session
.CreateQuery("update
versioned Product p set p.Price = p.Price * 2").ExecuteUpdate();
```

 Tip: Never update a version column by hand. Use protected setters to ensure this.

Batch Insertions

NHibernate is no ETL tool, which means it wasn't designed for bulk loading of data. Having said that, this doesn't mean it is impossible to do. However, the performance may not be comparable to other solutions. Still, there are some things we can do to help.

First, in modern databases, there is no need to insert one record at a time. Typically, these engines allow batching, which means that several records are inserted at the same time, thus minimizing the number of roundtrips. As you can guess, NHibernate supports insert batching; you just have to tell it to use it. Using loquacious configuration, we set the **BatchSize** and **Batcher** properties:

```
Configuration cfg = BuildConfiguration()
.DataBaseIntegration(db =>
{
  //...
  db.Batcher<SqlClientBatchingBatcherFactory>();
  db.BatchSize = 100;
})
```

 Tip: You need to add a reference to the NHibernate.AdoNet *namespace for the* SqlClientBatchingBatcherFactory *class.*

Or, if you prefer to use XML configuration, add the following properties to your **App/Web.config**:

```
<session-factory>
  <!-- ... -->
  <property name="adonet.factory_class">
NHibernate.AdoNet.SqlClientBatchingBatcherFactory, NHibernate</property>
  <property name="adonet.batch_size">100</property>
</session-factory>
```

Batcher factories exist for SQL Server and Oracle; the one for the latter is called **OracleDataClientBatchingBatcherFactory**. It is certainly possible to implement them for other engines and some people, in fact, have. It is a matter of implementing **IBatcherFactory** and **IBatcher**. Granted, it's not simple but it's still possible.

What the **BatchSize/batch-size** property means is, when inserting records, NHibernate should insert records 100 at a time instead of one by one.

For example, try the following example with and without batching enabled (set **BatchSize** to **0** and remove the **Batcher** declaration in the configuration):

```
Stopwatch watch = new Stopwatch();
watch.Start();

using (ISession session = sessionFactory.OpenSession())
using (session.BeginTransaction())
{
  for (Int32 i = 0; i < 1000; ++i)
  {

session.Save(new Product() { Name = String.Format("Product {0}", i), Price = (i + 1)
 * 10,
Specification = XDocument.Parse("<data/>") });

    if ((i % 100) == 0)
    {
```

```
        session.Flush();
        session.Clear();
    }
}

session.Transaction.Commit();
}

Int64 time = watch.ElapsedMilliseconds;
```

NHibernate has a lightweight alternative to the regular sessions called stateless sessions. Stateless sessions are built from a session factory and have some drawbacks:

- No first-level cache, which means stateless sessions do not know what changed.
- No cascading support.
- No lazy loading support.
- Fine-grained control over inserts and updates.
- No flushing; commands are sent immediately.
- No events are raised.

The same example with stateless sessions would look like this:

```
using (IStatelessSession session = sessionFactory.OpenStatelessSession())
using (session.BeginTransaction())
{
    for (Int32 i = 0; i < 1000; ++i)
    {

session.Insert(new Product() { Name = String.Format("Product {0}", i), Price
    = (i + 1) * 10,
Specification = XDocument.Parse("<data/>") });
    }

    session.Transaction.Commit();
}
```

Chapter 7 Restrictions and Filters

Restrictions

It is possible to specify additional restraining conditions to entities, which NHibernate always respects when performing SELECTs. These conditions come in two flavors: restrictions and filters. Let's first focus on restrictions.

A restriction is a static WHERE clause that can be added at class and collection levels (**sets**, **lists**, **bags**, **maps**, **id bags**, **arrays**, and **primitive arrays**) in order to filter its elements. A typical example would be soft deletes where records are not actually deleted from the database but, instead, are marked with a column value that represents deletion. Here's how we define this as XML, for classes and collections:

```
<class name="Blog" lazy="true" table="`POST`" where="deleted = 0">
  <!-- ... -->
  <list cascade="all-delete-orphan" inverse="true" lazy="true" name="Posts"
where="deleted = 0">
    <!-- ... -->
  </list>
</class>
```

Here is the equivalent code in mapping by code:

```
mapper.Class<Blog>(ca =>
{
  ca.Where("deleted = 0");
  //...

  ca.List(c => c.Posts, c =>
  {
    c.Where("deleted = 0");
    //...
  });
}
```

And in attributes:

```
[Class(Table = "blog", Lazy = true, Where = "deleted = 0")]
public class Blog
{
  //...
  [List(0, Inverse = true, Lazy = CollectionLazy.True, Generic = true,
Where = "deleted = 0", Cascade = "all-delete-orphan")]
  public virtual IList<Post> Posts { get; protected set; }
}
```

Whenever you query for the **Blog** entity, the "deleted = 0" restriction will be added automatically, even if you include other conditions:

```
IEnumerable<Blog> nonDeletedBlogs = session.Query<Blog>();
Blog b = session.Get<Blog>(1);
```

See the resulting SQL for the two queries:

```
SELECT
    blog0_.blog_id AS blog1_11_,
    blog0_.picture AS picture11_,
    blog0_.user_id AS user3_11_,
    blog0_.name AS name11_,
    blog0_.creation AS creation11_,
    (SELECT
        COUNT(1)
    FROM
        post
    WHERE
        post.blog_id = blog0_.blog_id) AS formula2_
FROM
    blog blog0_
WHERE
    (
    blog0_.deleted = 0
    )

SELECT
    blog0_.blog_id AS blog1_11_0_,
    blog0_.picture AS picture11_0_,
    blog0_.user_id AS user3_11_0_,
    blog0_.name AS name11_0_,
    blog0_.creation AS creation11_0_,
    (SELECT
        COUNT(1)
    FROM
        post
    WHERE
        post.blog_id = blog0_.blog_id) AS formula2_0_
FROM
    blog blog0_
WHERE
    blog0_.blog_id = 1
    AND
    (
    blog0_.deleted = 0
    )
```

Filters

A filter is similar to a restriction but it is dynamic. This means it can be enabled or disabled and can have parameters. One example might be a model in which you have translations of terms to multiple languages:

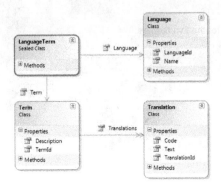

Figure 27: Translations Class Model

What we have is:

- A **Language**
- A **Term** with a collection of **Translations**
- A **Translation** of a **Term** for a given **Language**

This introduces a new concept: a class that maps a composite key. In this case, it is the **LanguageTerm** that contains a reference to both a **Term** and a **Language**.

Typically, you would use a model like this if you only want to load the translations for the current language, not for all of them. Its mappings might look like this:

```
public class LanguageMapping : ClassMapping<Language>
{
  public LanguageMapping()
  {
    this.Table("language");
    this.Lazy(true);

    this.Id(x => x.LanguageId, x =>
    {
      x.Column("language_id");
      x.Generator(Generators.Assigned);
    });

    this.Property(x => x.Name, x =>
    {
      x.Column("name");
      x.NotNullable(true);
      x.Length(100);
    });
  }
}
```

```csharp
public class TermMapping : ClassMapping<Term>
{
  public TermMapping()
  {
    this.Table("term");
    this.Lazy(true);

    this.Id(x => x.TermId, x =>
    {
      x.Column("term_id");
      x.Generator(Generators.HighLow);
    });

    this.Property(x => x.Description, x =>
    {
      x.Column("description");
      x.NotNullable(true);
      x.Length(50);
    });

    this.Set(x => x.Translations, x =>
    {
      x.Key(y =>
      {
        y.Column("term_id");
        y.NotNullable(true);
      });

      x.Filter("CurrentLanguage", z =>
      {
          z.Condition("language_id = :code");
      });

      x.Inverse(true);
      x.Cascade(Cascade.All | Cascade.DeleteOrphans);
      x.Lazy(CollectionLazy.Lazy);
    }, x =>
    {
      x.OneToMany();
    });
  }
}


public class TranslationMapping : ClassMapping<Translation>
{
  public TranslationMapping()
  {
    this.Table("translation");
    this.Lazy(true);

    this.Filter("CurrentLanguage", x =>
```

```
    {
        x.Condition("language_id = :code");
    });

    this.ComponentAsId(x => x.TranslationId, x =>
    {
      x.ManyToOne(y => y.Language, y =>
      {
        y.Column("language_id");
      });
      x.ManyToOne(y => y.Term, y =>
      {
        y.Column("term_id");
      });
    });

    this.Property(x => x.Text, x =>
    {
      x.Column("text");
      x.Length(100);
      x.NotNullable(true);
    });
  }
}
```

And, last but not least, a filter declaration, which must go on the **Configuration** instance before a session factory is built:

```
cfg.AddFilterDefinition(new FilterDefinition("CurrentLanguage", "language_id
  = :code",
new Dictionary<String, IType>() { { "code", NHibernateUtil.String } }, false
));
```

 Tip: Import namespaces NHibernate.Type *and* NHibernate.Engine.

Notice this:

- The **CurrentLanguage** filter is basically a restriction on a **language_id** column and it uses a **code** parameter.
- The primary key of the **Language** class, **LanguageId**, is a **String** and uses the **Assigned** pattern. We will use it for storing meaningful culture names like "**en-us**" or "**pt-pt**" which must always be unique.
- The **Translations** collection of the **Term** class has the **CurrentLanguage** filter applied to it.
- The **Translation** class has a composite key (**ComponentAsId**) implemented by the **LanguageTerm** class which references both a **Term** and a **Language**.
- The **Translation** class also uses the **CurrentLanguage** filter.

We need to assign a value to the **code** parameter of the filter and enable it before actually querying:

```
//set the filter value from the current thread's culture name
session.EnableFilter("CurrentLanguage").SetParameter("code", Thread.CurrentT
hread.CurrentCulture.Name);

var term = session.Query<Term>().First();

//the translations will be filtered
var translations = term.Translations.ToList();
```

The filter will be included in the SQL as a parameter:

```
SELECT
    TOP (1)  term0_.term_id AS term1_8_,
    term0_.description AS descript2_8_
FROM
    term term0_

SELECT
    translatio0_.term_id AS term2_1_,
    translatio0_.language_id AS language1_1_,
    translatio0_.language_id AS language1_9_0_,
    translatio0_.term_id AS term2_9_0_,
    translatio0_.text AS text9_0_
FROM
    [translation] translatio0_
WHERE
    translatio0_.language_id = 'en-us'
    AND translatio0_.term_id = 1
```

When you no longer need the filter, you just disable it:

```
//disable the filter
session.DisableFilter("CurrentLanguage");
```

Final notes:

- Each entity and collection may have several filters and more than one can be enabled at the same time.
- A filter may or may not have parameters and these can have default values.
- A filter may be enabled or disabled.
- A filter's SQL can only reference columns directly accessible by the class where it is applied.

Chapter 8 Interceptors and Listeners

Interceptors

In this chapter, we will look at what NHibernate has to offer when it comes to changing some of its default behavior and getting notified when some events occur.

NHibernate offers a mechanism by which we can intercept, among others:

- The creation of the SQL queries that will be sent to the database.
- The instantiation of entity classes.
- The indication if an entity should be persisted.
- The detection of the dirty properties.

Interceptors are a complex mechanism. Let's look at two simple examples—one for changing the SQL and the other for injecting behavior dynamically into entity classes loaded from records.

An interceptor is injected on the **Configuration** instance; only one can be applied at a time and that must be before building the session factory.

A typical implementation of a custom interceptor might inherit from the **NHibernate.EmptyInterceptor** class which is a do-nothing implementation of the **NHibernate.IInterceptor** interface:

```
public class SendSqlInterceptor : EmptyInterceptor
{
  private readonly Func<String> sqlBefore = null;
  private readonly Func<String> sqlAfter = null;

  public SendSqlInterceptor(Func<String> sqlBefore, Func<String> sqlAfter = null)
  {
    this.sqlBefore = sqlBefore;
    this.sqlAfter = sqlAfter;
  }

  public override SqlString OnPrepareStatement(SqlString sql)
  {
    sql = sql.Insert(0, String.Format("{0};", this.sqlBefore()));

    if (this.sqlAfter != null)
    {
      sql = sql.Append(String.Format(";{0}", this.sqlAfter()));
    }

    return (base.OnPrepareStatement(sql));
  }
}
```

Tip: *You need to reference the* NHibernate.SqlCommand *namespace for the* SqlString *class.*

This simple example allows you to send SQL commands before and, optionally, after any other:

```
cfg.SetInterceptor(new SendSqlInterceptor(() => "SET TRANSACTION ISOLATION L
EVEL READ UNCOMMITTED",
() => "DECLARE @msg NVARCHAR(100) = 'Query run at ' + CAST(GETDATE() AS VARC
HAR) + ' with ' + @@ROWCOUNT + ' records'; EXEC xp_logevent 60000, @msg, 0")
);
```

For more complex scenarios, you would have to parse the **SqlString** parameter and either insert, remove or replace any contents on your own.

A more interesting example is making use of NHibernate's built-in proxy generator—the one it uses to build lazy loading proxies. This is a way to automatically add a proper implementation of **INotifyPropertyChanged**. You might be familiar with this interface, which is used, for example, in WPF data binding where a control needs to be notified of any changes that occur to its data source's properties so that it can redraw itself. Implementing **INotifyPropertyChanged** has absolutely no complexity but it is a lot of work if we have many properties. Besides that, it forces us to use backing fields for properties. Here is the code for an interceptor that makes all loaded entities implement **INotifyPropertyChanged**:

```
public sealed class NotifyPropertyChangedInterceptor : EmptyInterceptor
{

    class _NotifyPropertyChangedInterceptor : NHibernate.Proxy.DynamicProxy.IInt
erceptor
    {
        private PropertyChangedEventHandler changed = delegate { };
        private readonly Object target = null;

        public _NotifyPropertyChangedInterceptor(Object target)
        {
            this.target = target;
        }

        #region IInterceptor Members

        public Object Intercept(InvocationInfo info)
        {
            Object result = null;

            if (info.TargetMethod.Name == "add_PropertyChanged")
            {
PropertyChangedEventHandler propertyChangedEventHandler = info.Arguments[0]
as PropertyChangedEventHandler;
                this.changed += propertyChangedEventHandler;
            }
            else if (info.TargetMethod.Name == "remove_PropertyChanged")
            {
```

```
PropertyChangedEventHandler propertyChangedEventHandler = info.Arguments[0]
as PropertyChangedEventHandler;
        this.changed -= propertyChangedEventHandler;
      }
      else
      {
        result = info.TargetMethod.Invoke(this.target, info.Arguments);
      }

      if (info.TargetMethod.Name.StartsWith("set_") == true)
      {
String propertyName = info.TargetMethod.Name.Substring("set_".Length);

this.changed(info.Target, new PropertyChangedEventArgs(propertyName));
      }

      return (result);
    }

    #endregion
  }

  private ISession session = null;
  private static readonly ProxyFactory factory = new ProxyFactory();

  public override void SetSession(ISession session)
  {
    this.session = session;
    base.SetSession(session);
  }


public override Object Instantiate(String clazz, EntityMode entityMode, Obje
ct id)
  {

Type entityType = this.session.SessionFactory.GetClassMetadata(clazz).GetMap
pedClass(
entityMode);

Object target = this.session.SessionFactory.GetClassMetadata(entityType).Ins
tantiate(id,
entityMode);

Object proxy = factory.CreateProxy(entityType, new _NotifyPropertyChangedInt
erceptor(target),
typeof(INotifyPropertyChanged));

this.session.SessionFactory.GetClassMetadata(entityType).SetIdentifier(proxy
, id, entityMode);
    return (proxy);
  }
}
```

Tip: You need to reference the NHibernate, NHibernate.Type, System.ComponentModel, and System.Reflection namespaces.

Its registration is as simple as:

```
cfg.SetInterceptor(new NotifyPropertyChangedInterceptor());
```

And a sample usage:

```
Product p = session.Query<Product>().First();

INotifyPropertyChanged npc = p as INotifyPropertyChanged;
npc.PropertyChanged += delegate(Object sender, PropertyChangedEventArgs args
)
{
    //...
};

p.Price *= 10; //raises the NotifyPropertyChanged event
```

Granted, this code is a bit complex. Nevertheless, it isn't hard to understand:

- The **Instantiate** method is called when NHibernate is going to create an object instance for a record obtained from the database. In the base **EmptyInterceptor** class it just returns **null** by default so NHibernate knows it must create it by itself.
- In our own implementation, we ask NHibernate to create an instance the way it would normally do, by calling **IClassMetadata.Instantiate**.
- NHibernate's **ProxyFactory** will then create a new proxy for the desired class, have it implement **INotifyPropertyChanged**, and pass it an implementation of a proxy interceptor, **_NotifyPropertyChangedInterceptor**, which will handle all requests for **virtual** or **abstract** methods and properties and, in the event of a setter call (identified by the prefix **"set_"** or an event registration – **"add_"**) will execute some custom code.
- Because the generated proxy will be of a class that inherits from an entity's class, it must not be marked as **sealed** and all of its properties and methods must be **virtual**.

Listeners

Listeners are NHibernate's events; they allow us to be notified when something occurs. It turns out that NHibernate offers a very rich set of events that cover just about anything you might expect—from entity loading, deletion and saving, to session flushing and more.

Multiple listeners can be registered for the same event; they will be called synchronously at specific moments which are described in the following table. The table lists both the code name as well as the XML name of each event. I have also included the name of the property in the **Configuration.EventListeners** property where the listeners can be added by code.

The full list of events is:

Event	Description and Registration Property
Autoflush/auto-flush	Called when the session is flushed automatically (**AutoFlushEventListeners** property)
Create/create	Called when an instance is saved (**PersistEventListeners**)
CreateOnFlush/ create-onflush	Called when an instance is saved automatically by a **Flush** operation (**PersistOnFlushEventListeners**)
Delete/delete	Called when an entity is deleted by a call to **Delete** (**DeleteEventListeners**)
DirtyCheck/dirty-check	Called when a session is being checked for dirty entities (**DirtyCheckEventListeners**)
Evict/evict	Called when an entity is being evicted from a session (**EvictEventListeners**)
Flush/flush	Called when a **Flush** call occurs or a transaction commits, after **FlushEntity** is called for each entity in the session (**FlushEventListeners**)
FlushEntity/flush-entity	Called for each entity present in a session when it is flushed (**FlushEntityEventListeners**)
Load/load	Called when a session is loaded either by the **Get/Load** method or by a query, after events **PreLoad** and **PostLoad** (**LoadEventListeners**)
LoadCollection/ load-collection	Called when an entity's collection is being populated (**InitializeCollectionEventListeners**)

Event	Description and Registration Property
Lock/lock	Called when an entity and its associated record are being locked explicitly, either by an explicit call to the **Lock** method or by passing a **LockMode** in a query (**LockEventListeners**)
Merge/merge	Called when an existing entity is being merged with a disconnected one, usually by a call to **Merge** (**MergeEventListeners**)
{Pre/Post}CollectionRecreate/{pre/post}-collection-recreate	Called before/after a bag is being repopulated, after its elements have changed (**{Pre/Post}CollectionRecreateEventListeners**)
{Pre/Post}CollectionRemove/{pre/post}-collection-remove	Called before/after an entity is removed from a collection (**{Pre/Post}CollectionRemoveEventListeners**)
{Pre/Post}CollectionUpdate/{pre/post}-collection-update	Called before/after a collection was changed (**{Pre/Post}CollectionUpdateEventListeners**)
PostCommitDelete/ post-commit-delete	Called after a delete operation was committed (**PostCommitDeleteEventListeners**)
PostCommitInsert/ post-commit-insert	Called after an insert operation was committed (**PostCommitInsertEventListeners**)
PostCommitUpdate/ post-commit-update	Called after an update operation was committed (**PostCommitUpdateEventListeners**)
{Pre/Post}Delete/ {pre/post}-delete	Called before/after a delete operation (**{Pre/Post}DeleteEventListeners**)
{Pre/Post}Insert/{pre/post}-insert	Called before/after an insert operation (**{Pre/Post}InsertEventListeners**)

Event	Description and Registration Property
{Pre/Post}Load/{pre/post}-load	Called before/after a record is loaded and an entity instance is created ({Pre/Post}LoadEventListeners)
{Pre/Post}Update/{pre/post}-update	Called before/after an instance is updated ({Pre/Post}UpdateEventListeners)
Refresh/refresh	Called when an instance is refreshed (RefreshEventListeners)
Replicate/replicate	Called when an instance is being replicated (ReplicateEventListeners)
Save/save	Called when an instance is being saved, normally by a call to Save or SaveOrUpdate but after PostInsert/PostUpdate (SaveEventListeners)
SaveUpdate/save-update	Called when an instance is being saved, normally by a call to SaveOrUpdate but after PostUpdate (SaveOrUpdateEventListeners)
Update/update	Called when an instance is being updated explicitly, by a call to Update (UpdateEventListeners)

An event listener needs to be registered in the **Configuration** instance prior to creating a session factory from it:

```
//register a listener for the FlushEntity event
cfg.AppendListeners(ListenerType.FlushEntity, new IFlushEntityEventListener[
]{
new ProductCreatedListener() });
```

It is also possible to register event handlers by XML configuration; make sure you add an assembly qualified type name:

```
<session-factory>
  <!-- ... -->
  <listener type="flush-
entity" class="Succinctly.Console.ProductCreatedListener, Succinctly.Console
"/>
</session-factory>
```

Let's look at two examples, one for firing a domain event whenever a new product is added and the other for adding auditing information to an entity.

Here's the first listener:

```csharp
public class ProductCreatedListener : IFlushEntityEventListener
{
    public static event Action<Product> ProductCreated;

    #region IFlushEntityEventListener Members

    public void OnFlushEntity(FlushEntityEvent @event)
    {
        if (@event.Entity is Product)
        {
            if (ProductCreated != null)
            {
                ProductCreated(@event.Entity as Product);
            }
        }
    }

    #endregion
}
```

 Tip: Add a using declaration for namespace *NHibernate.Event.*

An example usage:

```csharp
//register a handler for the ProductCreated event
ProductCreatedListener.ProductCreated += delegate(Product p)
{
    Console.WriteLine("A new product was saved");
};

//register a listener for the FlushEntity event
cfg.AppendListeners(ListenerType.FlushEntity, new IFlushEntityEventListener[
]{
new ProductCreatedListener() });

//a sample product
Product product = new Product() { Name = "Some Product", Price = 100, Specif
ication =
XDocument.Parse("<data/>") };

//save the new product
session.Save(product);
session.Flush();        //the ProductCreatedListener.ProductCreated event
will be raised here
```

As for the auditing, let's start by defining a common interface:

```
public interface IAuditable
{
  String CreatedBy { get; set; }
  DateTime CreatedAt { get; set; }
  String UpdatedBy { get; set; }
  DateTime UpdatedAt { get; set; }
}
```

The **IAuditable** interface defines properties for storing the name of the user who created and last updated a record, as well as the date and time of its creation and last modification. The concept should be familiar to you. Feel free to add this interface to any of your entity classes.

Next, the listener that will handle NHibernate events and fill in the auditing information:

```
public class AuditableListener : IFlushEntityEventListener, ISaveOrUpdateEve
ntListener,
IMergeEventListener
{
  public AuditableListener()
  {
    this.CurrentDateTimeProvider = () => DateTime.UtcNow;
    this.CurrentIdentityProvider = () => WindowsIdentity.GetCurrent().Name;
  }

  public Func<DateTime> CurrentDateTimeProvider { get; set; }
  public Func<String> CurrentIdentityProvider { get; set; }

  protected void ExplicitUpdateCall(IAuditable trackable)
  {
    if (trackable == null)
    {
      return;
    }

    trackable.UpdatedAt = this.CurrentDateTimeProvider();
    trackable.UpdatedBy = this.CurrentIdentityProvider();

    if (trackable.CreatedAt == DateTime.MinValue)
    {
      trackable.CreatedAt = trackable.UpdatedAt;
      trackable.CreatedBy = trackable.UpdatedBy;
    }
  }

  protected Boolean HasDirtyProperties(FlushEntityEvent @event)
  {
    if ((@event.EntityEntry.RequiresDirtyCheck(@event.Entity) == false)
|| (@event.EntityEntry.ExistsInDatabase == false) || (@event.EntityEntry.Loa
dedState == null))
    {
      return (false);
    }

    Object[] currentState = @event.EntityEntry.Persister
```

```
.GetPropertyValues(@event.Entity, @event.Session.EntityMode);
    Object[] loadedState = @event.EntityEntry.LoadedState;

return (@event.EntityEntry.Persister.EntityMetamodel.Properties.Where((prope
rty, i) =>

(LazyPropertyInitializer.UnfetchedProperty.Equals(currentState[i]) == false)

&& (property.Type.IsDirty(loadedState[i], currentState[i], @event.Session) =
= true))
    .Any());
}

  public void OnFlushEntity(FlushEntityEvent @event)
  {
if ((@event.EntityEntry.Status == Status.Deleted) || (@event.EntityEntry.Sta
tus == Status.ReadOnly))
    {
      return;
    }

    IAuditable trackable = @event.Entity as IAuditable;

    if (trackable == null)
    {
      return;
    }

    if (this.HasDirtyProperties(@event) == true)
    {
      this.ExplicitUpdateCall(trackable);
    }
  }

  public void OnSaveOrUpdate(SaveOrUpdateEvent @event)
  {
    IAuditable auditable = @event.Entity as IAuditable;

    if ((auditable != null) && (auditable.CreatedAt == DateTime.MinValue))
    {
      this.ExplicitUpdateCall(auditable);
    }
  }

  public void OnMerge(MergeEvent @event)
  {
    this.ExplicitUpdateCall(@event.Entity as IAuditable);
  }

  public void OnMerge(MergeEvent @event, IDictionary copiedAlready)
  {
    this.ExplicitUpdateCall(@event.Entity as IAuditable);
  }
}
```

As for the registration code, it is a little more complex than the previous example:

```
AuditableListener listener = new AuditableListener();
cfg.AppendListeners(ListenerType.Save, new ISaveOrUpdateEventListener[] { li
stener });
cfg.AppendListeners(ListenerType.SaveUpdate, new ISaveOrUpdateEventListener[
] { listener });
cfg.AppendListeners(ListenerType.Update, new ISaveOrUpdateEventListener[] {
listener });
cfg.AppendListeners(ListenerType.FlushEntity,
new IFlushEntityEventListener[] { listener });
cfg.AppendListeners(ListenerType.Merge, new IMergeEventListener[] { listener
 });
```

In XML:

```
<listener type="save" class="Succinctly.Common.AuditableListener, Succinctly
.Common"/>
<listener type="save-
update" class="Succinctly.Common.AuditableListener, Succinctly.Common"/>
<listener type="update" class="Succinctly.Common.AuditableListener, Succinct
ly.Common"/>
<listener type="flush-
entity" class="Succinctly.Common.AuditableListener, Succinctly.Common"/>
<listener type="merge" class="Succinctly.Common.AuditableListener, Succinctl
y.Common"/>
```

The **AuditableListener** class allows you to specify a delegate property for obtaining the current date and time (**CurrentDateTimeProvider**) and the name of the current user (**CurrentIdentityProvider**). It must be registered as a listener for several events (**Save**, **SaveOrUpdate**, **Update**, **FlushEntity**, and **Merge**) because several things can happen:

- An entity can be marked for saving (**Save**).
- An entity can be marked for saving or updating (**SaveOrUpdate**).
- An entity can be updated explicitly (**Update**).
- A disconnected entity may be merged with an existing one, thus possibly changing it (**Merge**).
- An entity that is dirty may reach a session flush (**FlushEntity**).

Chapter 9 Validation

NHibernate Validator

A proper data framework allows you to validate entities against business rules and invalid values. NHibernate Validator can be used precisely for that. It is a general purpose validation framework that integrates tightly with NHibernate.

The best way to get it is through NuGet as NHibernate.Validator:

```
PM> Install-Package NHibernate.Validator
```

Another way to get it is by downloading it from SourceForge:
http://sourceforge.net/projects/nhcontrib/files/NHibernate.Validator.

You can also get the source code from GitHub: https://github.com/darioquintana/NHibernate-Validator.

Once you have set it up, you must decide how you want to apply validation. NHibernate Validator supports configuring validation:

- By attributes.
- By XML.
- By code.

You see, some things in the NHibernate world never change!

To use NHibernate Validator, we need to set up the framework to work together with NHibernate. This is achieved through a listener that performs validation on entities when they are about to be saved or updated. If any validation error occurs, an **InvalidStateException** is thrown. You can call its **GetInvalidValues()** to find out exactly what is wrong and fix it.

We integrate NHibernate Validator with the NHibernate **Configuration** instance before building any session factory. The following shows how to do it with loquacious configuration:

```
FluentConfiguration validatorConfiguration = new FluentConfiguration();
validatorConfiguration.SetDefaultValidatorMode(ValidatorMode.UseExternal)
.IntegrateWithNHibernate.ApplyingDDLConstraints().RegisteringListeners();

NHibernate.Validator.Cfg.Environment.SharedEngineProvider = new NHibernateSh
aredEngineProvider();

ValidatorEngine validatorEngine = NHibernate.Validator.Cfg.Environment.Share
dEngineProvider.GetEngine();
validatorEngine.Configure(validatorConfiguration);
```

```
cfg.Initialize(validatorEngine);
```

 Tip: Add using statements for the NHibernate.Validator.Cfg.Loquacious, NHibernate.Validator, **and** NHibernate.Validator.Engine **namespaces.**

But it is also possible to do it with XML configuration; just make sure you add the following content to your **App/Web.config** file:

```
<configuration>
  <configSections>
    <!-- ... -->
    <section name="nhv-
configuration" type="NHibernate.Validator.Cfg.ConfigurationSectionHandler, N
Hibernate.Validator" />
  </configSections>
  <nhv-configuration xmlns="urn:nhv-configuration-1.0">
    <property name="apply_to_ddl">true</property>
    <property name="autoregister_listeners">true</property>
    <property name="default_validator_mode">UseExternal</property>
    <mapping assembly="Succinctly.Model"/>
  </nhv-configuration>
  <!-- ... -->
</configuration>
```

And include the following code:

```
XmlConfiguration xmlConfiguration = new XmlConfiguration();

ValidatorEngine validatorEngine = NHibernate.Validator.Cfg.Environment.Share
dEngineProvider.GetEngine();
validatorEngine.Configure(validatorConfiguration);

cfg.Initialize(validatorEngine);
```

If you want, you can also have IntelliSense for the NHibernate Validator XML. If you added NHibernate Validator from NuGet, just copy the **nhv-configuration.xsd** and **nhv-mapping.xsd** files from the **packages\NHibernate.Validator.1.3.2.4000\lib\Net35** folder to the **C:\Program Files (x86)\Microsoft Visual Studio 10.0\Xml\Schemas** or **C:\Program Files (x86)\Microsoft Visual Studio 11.0\Xml\Schemas**, depending on your Visual Studio version. See XML Configuration for more information on this. If you haven't used NuGet, you will have to extract these files from the distribution .zip file or the source GitHub repository.

Next, we need to configure validations for our entities. First, using code:

```
FluentConfiguration validatorConfiguration = new FluentConfiguration();
validatorConfiguration.Register(new CustomerValidation()).SetDefaultValidato
rMode(ValidatorMode.UseAttribute)
.IntegrateWithNHibernate.ApplyingDDLConstraints().RegisteringListeners();
```

The **CustomerValidation** class inherits from **NHibernate.Validator.ValidationDef<T>** and is defined as follows:

```
public class CustomerValidation : ValidationDef<Customer>
{
  public CustomerValidation()
  {
    this.ValidateInstance.By((customer, context) => customer.Address !=
null && /* something else */ )
.WithMessage("The customer address is mandatory");

this.Define(x => x.Name).NotNullableAndNotEmpty().WithMessage("The customer
name is mandatory");

this.Define(x => x.Name).MaxLength(50).WithMessage("The customer name can on
ly have 50 characters");

this.Define(x => x.Email).NotNullableAndNotEmpty().WithMessage("The customer
 email is mandatory");

this.Define(x => x.Email).MaxLength(50).WithMessage("The customer email can
only have 50 characters");

this.Define(x => x.Email).IsEmail().WithMessage("The customer email must be
a valid email adddress");
  }
}
```

And the same rules, except the **ValidateInstanceBy** custom validation can be defined in attributes like this:

```
public class Customer
{
  [NotNullNotEmpty(Message = "The customer name is mandatory")]

[Length(Max = 50, Message = "The customer name can only have 50 characters")
]
  public virtual String Name { get; set; }

  [NotNullNotEmpty(Message = "The customer email is mandatory")]
  [Email(Message = "The customer email must be a valid email adddress")]

[Length(Max = 50, Message = "The customer email can only have 50 characters"
)]
  public virtual String Email { get; set; }

  [NotNull(Message = "The customer address is mandatory")]
  public virtual Address Address { get; set; }
}
```

 *Tip: You need to reference the namespace NHibernate.Validator.Constraints.*

You have to change the Validator configuration to use attributes:

```
FluentConfiguration validatorConfiguration = new FluentConfiguration();
validatorConfiguration.SetDefaultValidatorMode(ValidatorMode.UseAttribute)
.IntegrateWithNHibernate.ApplyingDDLConstraints().RegisteringListeners();
```

Finally, to use XML, you need to add a file named **Customer.nhv.xml**, place it in the same location as the **Customer** class, and mark it as an embedded resource, just as we saw on XML Mappings:

```
<?xml version="1.0" encoding="utf-8" ?>
<nhv-mapping namespace="Succinctly.Model" assembly="Succinctly.Model"
xmlns="urn:nhibernate-validator-1.0">
  <class name="Customer">
    <property name="Name">

<length max="50" message="The customer name can only have 50 characters"/>
      <notnull-notempty message="The customer name is mandatory"/>
    </property>
    <property name="Email">

<length max="50" message="The customer email can only have 50 characters"/>
      <notnull-notempty message="The customer email is mandatory"/>
      <email message="The customer email must be a valid email adddress"/>
    </property>
    <property name="Address">
      <not-null message="The customer address is mandatory"/>
    </property>
  </class>
</nhv-mapping>
```

You also have to tell NHibernate Validator to look for embedded resources explicitly:

```
FluentConfiguration validatorConfiguration = new FluentConfiguration();
validatorConfiguration.Register(new [] { typeof(Customer) })
.SetDefaultValidatorMode(ValidatorMode.UseExternal)
.IntegrateWithNHibernate.ApplyingDDLConstraints().RegisteringListeners();
```

For some properties, we are using the built-in validation mechanisms such as **NotNullableAndNotEmpty** and **IsEmail** whereas, in other cases, we are performing a custom check (the **Address** reference). Out-of-the-box validators include:

Included Validators

Validator	Type	Description
Digits/digits/decimalmax/ **Decimalmin**	Numbers, Strings	Validates the maximum number of digits/digits and fractional digits

Validator	Type	Description
FilePathExists/fileexists	Strings	Checks if a file path exists
GreaterThanOrEqualTo/min	Numbers	Checks if a number is greater or equal to a given value
HasValidElements/isvalid	Collections	Checks if all of the collections' elements are valid recursively
IncludedBetween/range	Numbers	Checks if a number is included within a range (inclusive)
IsCreditCardNumber/ Creditcardnumber	Strings	Checks if a string matches a credit card number
IsEAN/ean	Numbers, Strings	Checks if a string or number matches an EAN
IsEmail/email	Strings	Checks if a string is a valid e-mail address
IsFalse/assertfalse	Booleans	Checks that a boolean is false
IsIBAN/iban	Strings	Checks that a string is a valid IBAN
IsInTheFuture/future	Dates and Times	Checks that a date is in the future
IsInThePast/past	Dates and Times	Checks that a date is in the past
IsIP/ipaddress	Strings	Checks that a string is a valid IP address
IsNumeric/digits	Strings	Checks that a string is a valid number

Validator	Type	Description
IsTrue/asserttrue	Booleans	Checks that a boolean is true
IsValid/valid	Entities	Checks that an entity is valid recursively
LengthBetween/length	Strings	Checks that the length of a string is contained within given limits
LessThanOrEqualTo/max	Numbers	Checks that a number is less or equal to a given value
MatchWith/pattern	Strings	Check that a string matches a regular expression
MaxLength/length	Strings	Checks the maximum length of a string
MaxSize/size	Collections	Checks the maximum size of a collection
MinLength/length	Strings	Checks the minimum length of a string
MinSize/size	Collections	Checks the minimum size of a collection
NotEmpty/not-empty	String, Collections, GUIDs	Checks if a string/collection/GUID is not empty
NotNullable/not-null	Any	Checks that a value is not null
NotNullableAndNotEmpty/ notnull-notempty	String, Collections	Checks that a string/collection is not null and contains values
Satisfy	Any	A custom rule, as a lambda expression

Validator	Type	Description
SizeBetween/size	Collections	Checks that a collection's size is contained within given limits
Whitih/range	Numbers	Checks if a number is included within a range (exclusive)

Some of these validations can be implemented on the database in the form of the maximum length for a string and as check constraints. In this case, if NHibernate Validator is integrated with NHibernate using the **ApplyingDDLConstraints/apply_to_ddl** option, when the model is generated, it will include these checks.

Finally, you can implement your own attributes by inheriting from **EmbeddedRuleArgsAttribute** and implementing a couple of interfaces:

```
[AttributeUsage(AttributeTargets.Property, AllowMultiple = false, Inherited
= true)]
public sealed class IsEvenAttribute : EmbeddedRuleArgsAttribute, IRuleArgs,
IValidator,
IPropertyConstraint
{
  public IsEvenAttribute()
  {
    this.Message = "Number is odd";
  }

  public String Message { get; set; }


public Boolean IsValid(Object value, IConstraintValidatorContext constraintV
alidatorContext)
  {
    Int32 number = Convert.ToInt32(value);

    return ((number % 2) == 0);
  }

  public void Apply(Property property)
  {
    Column column = property.ColumnIterator.OfType<Column>().First();
    column.CheckConstraint = String.Format("({0} % 2 = 0)", column.Name);
  }
}
```

This validator checks that a number is even, and can even change the property to which it is applied in order to add this check at the database level. That is what the **IPropertyConstraint** is for and you don't have to implement it because, sometimes, a validation cannot be expressed easily in database terms.

To add the attribute by XML, add a **<rule>** tag to **Customer.nhv.xml** that references your custom attribute:

```
<property name="SomeIntegerProperty">
  <rule attribute="IsEvenAttribute">
    <param name="Message" value="Number is odd"/>
  </rule>
</property>
```

Finally, let me just say this: Validation occurs when NHibernate tries to save an entity with validations attached but you can also validate explicitly:

```
InvalidValue[] invalidValuesObtainedExplicitly = validatorEngine.Validate(entity);
```

And that's just about it. Happy validating!

Chapter 10 Using NHibernate in Web Contexts

ASP.NET Web Forms

NHibernate is a general purpose persistence framework. It can be used in almost any .NET environment you can think of (but probably excluding Silverlight). However, in the case of ASP.NET web applications, there are some things that you might want to know to help your development process.

First, keep in mind that you will only ever need one session factory per application. Feel free to store it in a static variable; for example, in the **Global** class.

Second, one pattern that is common in web development is Open Session In View, which basically states that we should open a single session for each request, store it in an easy-to-find location, and keep it for the duration of the request, after which we can dispose of it. It is advisable that you follow this pattern. Let's see exactly how to do this.

NHibernate has the concept of the current session context. We are responsible for creating a session and binding it to this session context so that we can retrieve it later—even from different contexts (classes and methods). The session context implementation is specified by configuration, XML, or loquacious, and NHibernate includes the following implementations:

NHibernate Session Context Storage

Name	Purpose
CallSessionContext/call	The session is stored in the .NET Remoting **CallContext** class
ThreadStaticSessionContext/thread_static	The session is stored in a **ThreadStatic** variable
WcfOperationSessionContext/wcf_operation	The session is stored in the WCF **OperationContext** instance
WebSessionContext/web	The session is stored in the current **HttpContext**

Of course, for web applications, you would normally use the **WebSessionContext**. Here's how to set it up in XML and loquacious configuration:

```xml
<hibernate-configuration xmlns="urn:nhibernate-configuration-2.2">
  <session-factory>
    <!-- … -->
    <property name="current_session_context_class">web</property>
  </session-factory>
</hibernate-configuration>
```

```csharp
Configuration cfg = BuildConfiguration()
.DataBaseIntegration(db =>
{
  //…
})
.CurrentSessionContext<WebSessionContext>();
```

To properly implement the Open Session In View pattern, we need to hook up the **BeginRequest**, **EndRequest**, and **Error HttpApplication** events. This can be done in a module (IHttpModule) or in the **Global** class. Here's how it should look:

```csharp
public CurrentSessionContext SessionFactory { get; set; }

protected void OnBeginRequest(Object sender, EventArgs e)
{
  ISession session = this.SessionFactory.OpenSession();
  session.BeginTransaction();

  CurrentSessionContext.Bind(session);
}

protected void OnEndRequest(Object sender, EventArgs e)
{
  this.DisposeOfSession(true);
}

protected void OnError(Object sender, EventArgs e)
{
  this.DisposeOfSession(false);
}

protected void DisposeOfSession(Boolean commit)
{
  ISession session = CurrentSessionContext.Unbind(this.SessionFactory);

  if (session != null)
  {
if ((session.Transaction.IsActive == true) && (session.Transaction.WasCommitted == false)
    && (session.Transaction.WasRolledBack == false))
    {
```

```
    if (commit == true)
    {
        session.Transaction.Commit();
    }
    else
    {
        session.Transaction.Rollback();
    }

    session.Transaction.Dispose();
  }

  session.Dispose();
}
}
```

 Tip: Add a reference to the *NHibernate.Context* **namespace.**

Here's what it does:

1. When the **BeginRequest** event is raised, a session is created and stored in the current session context (**CurrentSessionContext.Bind()**), and a transaction is started.
2. When the **EndRequest** is raised, the session is retrieved (**CurrentSessionContext.Unbind()**) and disposed of, and the transaction is committed if it wasn't already.
3. If an **Error** occurs, the session is also disposed of and the active transaction is rolled back.

At any point, you can get the current session from the **ISessionFactory.GetCurrentContext()** method, but you need to have a pointer to the session factory for that:

```
ISession session = sessionFactory.GetCurrentSession();
```

If at any point in your code you need to cause the current transaction to roll back, just call the **Rollback** method of the **ITransaction** instance:

```
sessionFactory.GetCurrentSession().Rollback();
```

The code in the **EndRequest** handler will detect that the session was already rolled back and it won't do it again.

ASP.NET MVC

ASP.NET MVC uses an attribute-based approach for injecting cross-cutting behavior before and after action methods execute. This is generally referred to as Aspect-Oriented Programming (AOP) and, in MVC, it is called a filter. With this mechanism, you can easily start a session for the request and wrap each method in a transaction.

The following is the code for a simple filter that starts an NHibernate session (if it wasn't already started) and a transaction at the beginning of an action method and, after it finishes, commits the transaction and disposes of the session:

```
public class TransactionAttribute : ActionFilterAttribute, IExceptionFilter
{

public override void OnActionExecuting(ActionExecutingContext filterContext)
    {
    ISessionFactory
sessionFactory = DependencyResolver.Current.GetService<ISessionFactory>();

    if (CurrentSessionContext.HasBind(sessionFactory) == false)
    {
      CurrentSessionContext.Bind(sessionFactory.OpenSession());
    }

    if ((sessionFactory.GetCurrentSession().Transaction.IsActive == false))
    {
      sessionFactory.GetCurrentSession().BeginTransaction();
    }
  }

  public override void OnActionExecuted(ActionExecutedContext filterContext)
    {
    ISessionFactory
sessionFactory = DependencyResolver.Current.GetService<ISessionFactory>();
    if ((sessionFactory.GetCurrentSession().Transaction.IsActive == true)
      && (sessionFactory.GetCurrentSession().Transaction.WasCommitted == false)

&& (sessionFactory.GetCurrentSession().Transaction.WasRolledBack== false))
    {
      sessionFactory.GetCurrentSession().Transaction.Commit();
    }

    CurrentSessionContext.Unbind(sessionFactory).Dispose();
  }

  public void OnException(ExceptionContext filterContext)
    {

ISessionFactory sessionFactory = DependencyResolver.Current.GetService<ISessionFactory>();

    if ((sessionFactory.GetCurrentSession().Transaction.IsActive == true)
```

```
         && (sessionFactory.GetCurrentSession().Transaction.WasCommitted == false)

         && (sessionFactory.GetCurrentSession().Transaction.WasRolledBack== false))
            {
                sessionFactory.GetCurrentSection().Transaction.Rollback();
            }

            CurrentSessionContext.Unbind(sessionFactory).Dispose();
        }
}
```

 Tip: This example assumes that you have registered the *ISessionFactory* **with the** *DependencyResolver.*

WCF Web Services

When you use NHibernate to retrieve data in a web service, you must be aware of the following: If you use lazy loading for some property, reference or collection, and you leave the web method without explicitly loading everything, when your entity is serialized it will most likely not have access to the session from which it came. This is because it should have been disposed and so an exception will occur. Take the following code as an example of a bad implementation:

```
[OperationContract]
public IEnumerable<Product> GetProducts()
{
  using (ISession session = this.sessionFactory.OpenSession())
  {
    return (session.Query<Product>().ToList());
  }
}
```

If the **Product** entity is configured with any lazy properties, it will crash as soon as it is serialized because, by then, its originating session is closed.

A better implementation relies on a Data Transfer Object (DTO) that represents the data that we need to send, which typically is a subset or a transformation of the data exposed by the entity class:

```
[OperationContract]
public IEnumerable<Product> GetProducts()
{
  using (ISession session = this.sessionFactory.OpenSession())
  {
    return (session.Query<Product>().Select(x => new ProductDTO
```

```
            { Name = x.Name, Price = x.Price, Orders = x.OrderCount }).ToList());
    }
}
```

You can also use the same session context as you would normally use in a web application (the WCF session context is complex to set up and really doesn't introduce anything special), and also stick with the Open Session In View; you just have to make sure your WCF service is in ASP.NET Compatibility Mode (see http://msdn.microsoft.com/en-us/library/ms752234.aspx).

Chapter 11 Extending NHibernate

Extending LINQ

One common request is for the ability to have strongly typed LINQ expressions that take functions and have these functions run on the database. This is indeed possible with NHibernate. Let's take a look at how this is possible.

First, let's define a function prototype for something that we would like to call. In this example, I chose the SQL Server SOUNDEX function, for which you may find more information at http://msdn.microsoft.com/en-us/library/ms187384.aspx. Basically, this function returns a hash based on the sound that a string makes, thus allowing the successful comparison of badly written words. As far as the SOUNDEX algorithm is concerned, the following strings are the same:

- Ricardo.
- Riicardo.
- Ryicardo.

You can see it for yourself:

```
SELECT SOUNDEX('Ricardo')   --R263
SELECT SOUNDEX('Riicardo')  --R263
SELECT SOUNDEX('Rycardo')   --R263
```

If we wanted to call SOUNDEX in a LINQ query, we might define the following extension method on the **String** class:

```
public static class StringExtensions
{
  [LinqExtensionMethod]
  public static String Soundex(this String input)
  {
    throw new NotImplementedException();
  }
}
```

 Tip: Add a reference to the NHibernate.Linq namespace.

All we need to do to make it callable by NHibernate is to decorate it with the **[LinqExtensionMethod]** attribute from the **NHibernate.Linq** namespace. We can now write code like this and have NHibernate translate it to the appropriate SQL:

```
String soundexName = session.Query<Customer>().Select(x => x.Name.Soundex())
  .First();
```

Because the SOUNDEX method has no .NET implementation, we know that it is running in the database.

NHibernate already includes a useful extension for performing LIKE comparisons:

```
IEnumerable<Product> products = session.Query<Product>().Where(x => SqlMethods.Like(x.Name,
"%phone%"))
.ToList();
```

So, to clarify, we can apply the **[LinqExtensionMethod]** to any .NET method for which there is a corresponding SQL function with the same name and parameter signatures. There is no need to implement this method in .NET but, if you are curious, there is a possible implementation of the SOUNDEX algorithm in this book's companion code. You can also find plenty of information about it on the Internet.

Extending HQL

Like LINQ, we can also extend HQL so that it knows any database-specific functions that we would like to use. It is normally done by extending a **Dialect** class and registering those functions there, but it is also very easy to achieve by reflection:

```
public static class SessionFactoryExtensions
{
public static ISQLFunction RegisterFunction<T>(this ISessionFactory factory,
  String name, String sql)
  {
    MethodInfo registerFunctionMethod = typeof(Dialect)
.GetMethod("RegisterFunction", BindingFlags.Instance | BindingFlags.NonPubli
c);
    Dialect dialect = (factory as SessionFactoryImpl).Dialect;
    IType type = NHibernateUtil.GuessType(typeof(T));
    ISQLFunction function = new SQLFunctionTemplate(type, sql);
    registerFunctionMethod.Invoke(dialect, new Object[] { name, function });

    return (function);
  }
}
```

 Tip: Reference namespaces System.Reflection, NHibernate, NHibernate.Dialect, NHibernate.Dialect.Function, NHibernate.Impl, and NHibernate.Dialect.

One reason why you would follow this approach instead of subclassing **Dialect** is, if you need to support multiple databases, you would have to subclass all of their dialects' classes.

As an example, using SQL Server's **DATEADD** and **GETDATE** functions:

```
sessionFactory.RegisterFunction<DateTime>("last_week", "DATEADD(DAY, -
7, GETDATE())");

using (ISession session = sessionFactory.OpenSession())
{
    IEnumerable<Order> recentOrders = session
.CreateQuery("from Order o where o.Date >= last_week()")
.List<Order>();
}
```

Chapter 12 Monitoring NHibernate

log4net Integration

NHibernate has out-of-the-box integration with log4net, a general purpose and widely used logging framework. If you added the NHibernate support from NuGet, you already have log4net because it is a required dependency. If not, do add a reference to it, preferably with NuGet:

```
PM> Install-Package log4net
```

Otherwise, navigate to http://logging.apache.org/log4net and download the latest binaries.

Either way, configure your NHibernate environment to use log4net instead of its own logging facility, which you should disable. The configuration file **Web/App.config** should have a section like this:

```
<configSections>

<section name="log4net" type="log4net.Config.Log4NetConfigurationSectionHand
ler, log4net" />
  <section name="hibernate-configuration"
type="NHibernate.Cfg.ConfigurationSectionHandler, NHibernate" />
</configSections>
<log4net debug="false">
  <appender name="trace" type="log4net.Appender.ConsoleAppender, log4net">
    <layout type="log4net.Layout.PatternLayout, log4net">
      <param name="ConversionPattern" value="%d{ABSOLUTE} %-
5p %c{1}:%L - %m%n" />
    </layout>
  </appender>
  <logger name="NHibernate.SQL">
    <level value="DEBUG" />
      <priority value="DEBUG" />
      <appender-ref ref="trace" />
  </logger>
</log4net>
<hibernate-configuration xmlns="urn:nhibernate-configuration-2.2">
  <session-factory>
    <property name="format_sql">true</property>
    <property name="show_sql">false</property>
  </session-factory>
</hibernate-configuration>
```

For web applications, replace the **ConsoleAppender** with the **TraceAppender** to use the trace window instead of the console for the log output:

```
<appender name="trace" type="log4net.Appender.TraceAppender, log4net">
```

Now we just have to tell log4net to read its configuration and start producing output:

```
log4net.Config.XmlConfigurator.Configure();
```

NHibernate will output nicely formatted SQL for every query it sends to the database, including all parameters' types and values.

Statistics

Another nice feature is statistics. NHibernate keeps a count of virtually anything it does, at the session factory level. This means that for all sessions spawning from it, this information is available as the **ISessionFactory.Statistics** property. Some of the data available is:

- Creation timestamp of the session factory.
- Number of connections opened and closed.
- Number of entities loaded, deleted, updated, and inserted.
- Number of flush operations.
- Number of optimistic concurrency failures.
- Number of queries executed.
- Maximum query execution time.
- Number of total and successful transactions.
- Last queries executed.

Normally, statistics are enabled unless we disable them explicitly by configuration:

```
<property name="generate_statistics">false</property>
```

Or by code:

```
cfg.SetProperty(NHibernate.Cfg.Environment.GenerateStatistics, Boolean.False
String);
```

At any point, we can also reset all statistics to their initial values:

```
sessionFactory.Statistics.Clear();
```

Chapter 13 Performance Optimizations

Optimizing Queries

Here are some general tips for optimizing queries with NHibernate:

- Select only the properties you need; that is, avoid selecting the full entity when you don't need it.
- Avoid loading an entity when you only need its key (use **ISession.Load<T>** instead of **ISession.Get<T>**).
- Use paging instead of retrieving all records at the same time; all querying APIs support it.
- Fetch at query time all the references and collections that you will need.
- Choose lazy and eager loading carefully, and choose an appropriate fetch mode. If you are certain that you need a child collection's items each time you load a specific entity, mark this collection as not lazy and with fetch mode JOIN.
- Resort to SQL queries when performance is crucial.

Optimizing Making Changes

Consider this:

- Always use explicit transactions.
- Use executable HQL for bulk updates and deletes.
- Use batching and stateless sessions for insertions.
- Evict unneeded entities from the session.
- Mark entities that you never want to change as immutable so that the session does not waste time with them when tracking changes.
- Use explicit flushing and, when flushing, also clear the session or evict unneeded entities.
- In production, disable logging and statistics.

Chapter 14 Putting It All Together

Our journey with NHibernate has come to an end. I hope you have enjoyed reading this book as much as I have enjoyed writing it. By now, you should have a fairly good idea of NHibernate's potential as well as its limitations.

I think the most important subjects we talked about were:

- The various mapping techniques, collection alternatives, and querying APIs.
- The extensibility mechanisms, of which we barely scratched the surface.
- The listeners and interceptors, on which we can totally change the way NHibernate operates.
- The Validation API, which is very rich and extensible.

We barely scratched the surface, though. There is no better way to learn NHibernate than to actually work with it. So do your own experimentations, look at the source code, and tweak the various configuration settings.

With that said, I wish you a good experience. Remember to share your findings with others!

Chapter 15 Additional References

NHibernate Forge

NHibernate Forge can be found at http://nhforge.org; it is the central point of information on all things related to NHibernate. Here you will find announcements for new versions, blog and wiki posts, and links to official API reference documentation. Unfortunately, it's not always up to date but it's still a valuable source of information.

NHibernate Reference

NHibernate Reference is the ultimate source of information on the NHibernate usage and configuration. You can find it at http://nhforge.org/doc/nh/en.

NHibernate Validator Documentation

Find the reference documentation for NHibernate Validator at:
http://nhforge.org/wikis/validator/nhibernate-validator-1-0-0-documentation.aspx.

NHibernate Users

It may well happen that you'll face problems when using NHibernate or that you just won't know the best way to do something. In this case, one place you can turn to is the NHibernate Users community, which is available as a mailing list that's hosted at Google Groups (which offers a web interface: https://groups.google.com/forum/?fromgroups#!forum/nhusers). Here, you will find many users who work with NHibernate on a daily basis and who may be able to help you.

NHibernate Development

If you ever need to contact the NHibernate authors to discuss the implementation of NHibernate, there is the NHibernate Development community, also hosted at Google Groups: https://groups.google.com/forum/?fromgroups#!forum/nhibernate-development. You won't typically find solutions to your immediate problems here but, instead, you may learn from the conversations between the developers or you can discuss features with the people who actually built them.

NHibernate JIRA

NHibernate JIRA at https://nhibernate.jira.com is the place to go for filling bug reports, suggesting improvements, or looking up existing issues. If you are going to submit a bug report, please include the maximum amount of detail possible and make sure you carefully fill in all fields with appropriate values.

Figure 28: JIRA Interface

Even better, include a simple unit test that demonstrates the problem you are facing. You will find guidelines on writing good unit tests on this wiki post: http://nhforge.org/blogs/nhibernate/archive/2008/10/04/the-best-way-to-solve-nhibernate-bugs-submit-good-unit-test.aspx. A test project is available at http://nhforge.org/media/p/70.aspx.

NHibernate Source Code

NHibernate source code is available on GitHub at https://github.com/nhibernate/nhibernate-core.

NHibernate Validator Source Code

NHibernate Validator source code is also available on GitHub and maintained by Dario Quintana (@darioquintana) at https://github.com/darioquintana/NHibernate-Validator.

NHibernate Pitfalls Index

I keep my own list of common NHibernate pitfalls and recommendations on my blog at http://weblogs.asp.net/ricardoperes. Have a look and share your thoughts, questions, and corrections.

Contributing to NHibernate

Once you get familiar with NHibernate, including its source code, you may feel that you can bring something new to NHibernate, either by fixing existing bugs or by implementing new functionality. That is good because NHibernate is the product of a community of people who think that way. You are free to try and contribute to it. To do so, you must follow these steps:

1. Create an account on NHibernate JIRA if you don't already have one.
2. Create an issue for what you are trying fix or improve, if one does not already exist (including a unit test that illustrates the situation).
3. Read the Contributor Guide available at https://github.com/nhibernate/nhibernate-core/blob/master/Contributor%20Guide.html.
4. Fork the **nhibernate-core** repository from the GitHub web interface:

Figure 29: Creating a Pull Request

5. Clone the forked source code to your development machine from the command line:

Figure 30: Cloning a Repository

6. Run **ShowBuildMenu.bat** and select option **A** for setting up the development environment:

Figure 31: Setting Up Initial NHibernate Development Environment

7. Make changes to the code and make sure you don't break anything.
8. Commit your changes from the command line:

Figure 32: Committing Changes

9. Create a pull request from the web interface and fill in all required values:

Figure 33: Creating a Pull Request

10. Go to the JIRA issue and add a comment to it where you mention your proposed solution and the location of the pull request:

Figure 34: Mentioning the Pull Request on a JIRA Issue

11. Wait for someone on the NHibernate team to pick it up, test it, and merge your changes with the trunk.

www.ingramcontent.com/pod-product-compliance
Lightning Source LLC
Chambersburg PA
CBHW071247050326
40690CB00011B/2295